PHILOSOPHY
IN A WEEK

Mel Thompson

The Teach Yourself series has been trusted around the world
for over 60 years. This academic series of 'In A Week' books
is designed to help people at all levels and around the world
to discover the basics of key ideas in the fields of philosophy,
religion and culture. Learn in a week, remember for a lifetime.

Mel Thompson is a former teacher, lecturer and publisher, and today works as a freelance writer specializing in philosophy and ethics both for the general reader and the student. With Hodder & Stoughton he has published, among other titles, *Understand Philosophy, Understand Ethics, Eastern Philosophy and Philosophy of Mind*, all part of the highly regarded Teach Yourself series.

PHILOSOPHY

Mel Thompson

www.inaweek.co.uk

IN A WEEK

Teach Yourself®

First published in Great Britain in 2011 by Hodder & Stoughton. An Hachette UK company.

First published in US in 2011 by The McGraw-Hill Companies, Inc.

This revised and expanded edition published 2013

Previously published as *Philosophy Made Simple*

Copyright © Mel Thompson 2011, 2013

British Library Cataloguing in Publication Data: a catalogue record for this title is available from the British Library.

Library of Congress Catalog Card Number: on file.

10 9 8 7 6 5 4 3 2 1

The publisher has used its best endeavours to ensure that any Website addresses referred to in this book are correct and active at the time of going to press. However, the publisher and the author have no responsibility for the Websites and can make no guarantee that a site will remain live or that the content will remain relevant, decent or appropriate.

The publisher has made every effort to mark as such all words which it believes to be trademarks. The publisher should also like to make it clear that the presence of a word in the book, whether marked or unmarked, in no way affects its legal status as a trademark.

Every reasonable effort has been made by the publisher to trace the copyright holders of material in this book. Any errors or omissions should be notified in writing to the publisher, who will endeavour to rectify the situation for any reprints and future editions.

Artworks © Peter Lubach

Typeset by Cenveo® Publisher Services.

Printed and bound by CPI Group (UK) Ltd, Croydon, CR0 4YY

Hodder & Stoughton policy is to use papers that are natural, renewable and recyclable products and made from wood grown in sustainable forests. The logging and manufacturing processes are expected to conform to the environmental regulations of the country of origin.

Hodder & Stoughton Ltd

338 Euston Road

London NW1 3BH

www.hodder.co.uk

CONTENTS

INTRODUCTION

In order to enjoy philosophy, it is important to remember that it is both an activity and a body of knowledge.

As an activity, it is a matter of asking questions, challenging assumptions, re-examining traditionally held views, unpacking the meaning of words, weighing up the value of evidence and examining the logic of arguments. It cultivates an enquiring and critical mind, even if it sometimes infuriates those who want an easy intellectual life. Philosophy is also a means of clarifying your own thinking. The clearer your thought, the better able you will be to express yourself, and the more accurate your way of examining arguments and making decisions.

As a body of knowledge, it is the cumulative wisdom of great thinkers. It offers you a chance to explore fundamental questions and to see what thinkers in different periods of history have had to say about them. This in itself is valuable, because it frees you from being limited by the unquestioned assumptions of those around you. To think through issues from first principles is a natural result of having looked at the way in which philosophers have gone about their work. So this second aspect of philosophy reinforces the first.

Philosophy is a tool with which to expose nonsense, and express ideas in a way that is as unambiguous as possible. For example, philosophy makes a distinction between 'analytic' and 'synthetic' statements. An analytic statement is known to be true once the definitions of its terms are understood. $2 + 2 = 4$ is just such a statement. You don't have to go out gathering sets of two items and counting them in order to verify it. You cannot return triumphant and proclaim that you have found a single case which disproves the rule – that you have two sets of two which actually add up to five! Proof, for analytic statements, does not require research or experimental testing. On the other hand, if I say that a certain person is at home, that cannot be true in the same way – it is a synthetic statement, based on evidence. To find out whether or not it is true, you have to phone or visit. The statement can easily be proved wrong, and it certainly cannot be true for all time.

But if someone says 'God exists', is that an analytic or a synthetic statement? Can you define 'God' in such a way that his existence is inevitable? If so, can any evidence be relevant for or against that claim? You might argue that:

● God is everything that exists.
● Everything that exists, exists.
● Therefore God exists.

This argument is sound, but it implies that 'God' and 'everything that exists' are interchangeable terms. This is **pantheism** (the idea that God and the world are identical) and it is quite logical, but is it what most people mean by the word 'God'? And what are its implications for the way we see 'everything that exists'? We observe that everything in the world is liable to change. There will come a time when nothing that exists now will remain. Does this mean that a pantheistic god is also constantly changing? Does it make sense for a word to stay the same, when the thing to which it refers changes? Is a school the same if its buildings are replaced, its staff move on to other posts, and its pupils leave year by year to be replaced by others? Am I the same, even though most of the cells in my body are changing, and my thoughts are constantly on the move? What is the 'I' that remains throughout my life?

This illustrates another feature of philosophy, and a good reason to study it: you can start from any one question and find yourself drawn outwards to consider many others. Start with 'the self', and you find that matters of metaphysics or religion are drawn into your thinking. By using the skills of philosophy, you have the means of integrating your ideas, of relating them, and of testing them out within a wide range of issues.

Mel Thompson

SUNDAY

The theory of knowledge

Theory of knowledge examines what we know and how we know it. It asks whether knowledge starts with the mind or with the experience of our senses. Descartes famously claimed that the only thing we can know for certain is the fact of our own thinking ('I think, therefore I am'), whereas Hume argued that we should proportion our belief to our evidence, and Kant showed that our minds shape the way in which we experience the world.

Today we shall also look at the different views of Plato and Aristotle on whether general or ideal entities (e.g. justice, goodness) actually exist in themselves, or whether they are only summaries of the qualities we see in individual things.

In the end we need to consider whether we should be sceptical about our knowledge, or take a pragmatic view that we should assess our knowledge on the basis of what works.

FUNDAMENTAL QUESTIONS

There are two basic questions which have been asked throughout the history of philosophy and which affect the way in which many different topics are considered:

1 WHAT CAN WE KNOW?

This question is about the basic features of existence; not the sort of information that science gives about particular things, but the questions that lie beneath all such enquiry: questions about the fundamental nature of space, time or causality; about whether concepts like 'justice' or 'love' have any external, objective reality; about the structure of the world as we experience it. In the collected works of Aristotle, such questions were dealt with after his material on physics and were therefore called **metaphysics**.

But as soon as we start considering metaphysics, yet another question arises:

2 HOW CAN WE KNOW IT?

Is there anything of which we can be absolutely certain? Do we depend entirely on our senses, or can we discover basic truths simply by thinking? How can we justify or prove the truth of what we claim? All such questions are considered under **epistemology** – the theory of knowledge.

EMPIRICISM AND RATIONALISM

Within epistemology (the theory of knowledge) there is a fundamental issue about whether our knowledge originates in, and is therefore dependent upon, the data we receive through our senses, or whether (since we know that all such sense data are fallible) the only true certainties are those that come from our own minds – from the way in which we think and organize our experience, from the principles of reason and logic.

Two key terms:
- **empiricism** – all knowledge starts with the senses.
- **rationalism** – all knowledge starts with the mind.

However, the issue of experience and the way the mind categorizes it is far from straightforward. A very basic problem here concerns **reductionism**, and the existence of, or reality of, complex entities or general concepts.

Consider these questions:

- How does a painting relate to the individual pigments or threads of canvas of which is it made?
- How does music relate to vibrations in the air?
- How does a person relate to the individual cells in his or her body?
- How does a nation relate to the citizens of which it is made up?

A 'reductionist' approach to metaphysics takes the 'nothing but' view, for example that music is 'nothing but' vibrations in the air.

If you believe that the ultimate reality is matter – the solid external world that we experience through our senses – then you are probably going to call yourself a **materialist**. On the other hand, if you hold that the basic reality is mental – that the world of your experience is in fact the sum of all the sensations and perceptions that have registered in your mind – you may call yourself an **idealist**.

KNOWLEDGE AND JUSTIFICATION: ARE YOU CERTAIN?

Imagine that I am taken to a police station and questioned about something that is alleged to have happened in the recent past. I give my account of what I have heard or seen. If it sounds credible, or agrees with the evidence of others, I am likely to be believed. On the other hand, the police may ask, 'Are you sure about that? Is it possible that you were mistaken?' The implication is that, even if I am trying to be accurate and honest, the senses may be mistaken, and there may be two quite different ways of interpreting an experience.

When philosophers ask, 'What can be known for certain?' or 'Are the senses a reliable source of knowledge?' they are trying to sort out this element of uncertainty, so as to achieve statements that are known to be true.

Basically, as we saw above, there are two ways of approaching this problem, corresponding to the two elements in every experience:

1 Empiricists are those who start with the sensations of an experience, and say that all of our knowledge of the world is based on sensation.
2 Rationalists are those who claim that the basis of knowledge is the set of ideas we have – the mental element that sorts out and interprets experience. Rationalists consider the mind to be primary, and the actual data of experience to be secondary.

DESCARTES

René Descartes (1596–1650) placed one question centre stage: 'Of what can I be certain?' He used the method of systematic doubt, by which he would accept only what he could see clearly and distinctly to be true. He knew that his senses could be deceived, therefore he would not trust them, nor could he always trust his own logic. He realized that he might even be dreaming what he took to be a waking reality. His approach is one that will be examined below, in the discussion on scepticism. Yet the one thing Descartes could not doubt was his own existence. If he doubted, he was there to doubt; therefore he must exist. The famous phrase which expresses this is *cogito ergo sum* ('I think, therefore I am').

In many ways, Descartes' argument represents the starting point of modern philosophy (modern, that is, as compared to that of the ancient Greeks and of the medieval world), not because later thinkers have been in agreement with him but because, challenged by scepticism, they have followed his quest to find the basis of certainty and knowledge. In other words, Descartes set the theory of knowledge at the heart of the philosophical agenda.

PLATO

It has been said that the whole of Western philosophy is a set of footnotes to Plato (427–347 BCE), and there is a great deal of truth in that, since Plato covered a wide range of issues, and raised questions that have been debated ever since.

In *The Republic*, Plato uses an analogy to illustrate his view of human experience and his theory of knowledge. A row of prisoners sit near the back of a cave, chained so that they cannot turn to face its mouth. Behind them is a fire, in front of which are paraded various objects. The fire casts shadows of these objects on to the wall at the back of the cave, and this is all the prisoners can see. Plato thinks that this corresponds to the normal way in which things are experienced: shadows, not reality itself.

But Plato then presents a situation in which a prisoner is freed so that he can turn round and see the fire and the objects that cast the shadows. His first impression is that the objects are not as 'real' as those images he has been accustomed to seeing. But then he is forcibly dragged up to the mouth of the cave and into the sunlight and he gradually adjusts to the light of the sun. The experience of daylight and perceiving the sun is painful, and requires considerable adjustment. Only then does it become clear to the prisoner that his former perceptions were only shadows, not reality. This, for Plato, corresponds to the journey from seeing particular things, to seeing the eternal realities of which the particulars are mere shadow-like copies.

In Plato's dialogues, Socrates debates the meaning of words as a means of getting to understand the reality to which they point. So, for example, he argues that 'Justice' is not just a word that is used to bracket certain events and situations together. Justice actually exists, as a reality over and above any of the individual things that are said to be just. Indeed, the individual things can be said to be 'just' only because we already have knowledge of 'justice' itself and can see that they share in its reality.

These general realities he calls 'Forms'. If we did not have knowledge of such Forms we would have no ability to put anything into a category. The Form of something is its essential feature, the thing that makes it what it is.

ARISTOTLE

In the great legacy of Greek thought, Aristotle (384–322 BCE) offers an interesting contrast to Plato. Whereas Plato explored the world of the 'Forms', known only to the intellect – a perfect world, free from the limitations of the particular things we experience – Aristotle's philosophy is based on what is known through experience. He categorized the sciences (physics, psychology and economics all come from Aristotle) and gave us many of the terms and concepts that have dominated science and philosophy (including energy, substance, essence and category).

In rejecting Plato's Forms, Aristotle nevertheless acknowledged that people needed to consider 'sorts' of things, rather than each particular thing individually (try describing something without using general terms to indicate the kind of thing it is), but he believed that the Forms (to use Plato's term) were immanent in the particulars. In other words, I may look at a variety of things that are red, and say that what they have in common is redness. The quality 'redness' is actually part of my experience of those things. But what would it mean to have absolute redness; a redness that was not a red something or other? In Aristotle's philosophy, we do not go outside the world of experience in order to know the meaning of universal concepts; we simply apply them within experience.

Starting with experience

In the quest for knowledge, there are two contrasting approaches: one (rationalism) starts with the mind; the other (empiricism) starts with experience. The essential thing to grasp as we look at empiricism is that sense data (which make up the content of our experience) are not simply 'things' out there in the world. They depend upon our own faculties – the way in which we experience as well as what we experience.

The rationalism/empiricism debate can be seen by contrasting Descartes' views (as briefly outlined above) with those of John Locke, George Berkeley and David Hume, who are key figures in the development of empiricism.

LOCKE

John Locke (1632–1704) is known both for his empiricism, analysing sense experience and the way in which we learn, and also for his political philosophy. In his *Essay Concerning Human Understanding* (1689), he was on the same quest as Descartes: the desire to know what the mind can comprehend and what it cannot. But his conclusions were radically different. He claimed that there are no such things as innate ideas, and that all that we know comes to us from experience, and from reflecting upon experience.

Locke held that there are primary qualities (solidity, extension, motion, number) and secondary qualities (colour, sound, taste, etc.). The former inhere in bodies (i.e. they are independent of our perceiving them); the latter depend upon the act of perception (i.e. being able to see, hear, etc.).

BERKELEY

Bishop George Berkeley (1685–1753) was a fascinating character. He wrote his philosophy while in his twenties, later became a bishop, and took an interest in higher education in the American Colonies (where he lived for some time), leaving his library of books to Yale University.

Berkeley argued for **idealism**, which is the theory that everything that exists is mental. This sounds an unlikely view to hold about the world, but it follows from the way in which we perceive things. An idealist might argue as follows:

- All we actually know of the world are sensations (colour, sound, taste, touch, the relative positions of things that we perceive). We cannot know the world by any other means. For us, these sensations are what we mean by 'the world'.
- All these sensations are 'ideas': they are mental phenomena. (The colour red does not exist independent of the mind perceiving something of that colour.)
- Things are therefore collections of these ideas; they exist by being perceived.

Is the world all in our mind?

Berkeley also held that there are no abstract general ideas. If you think of a triangle, you are thinking of a particular triangle. It shares its qualities with other triangles, but there is no concept of triangle that does not spring from some particular triangle. What we think of as a 'universal' is just a set of qualities abstracted from particulars.

HUME

David Hume (1711–76) was a popular and radical philosopher and man of letters who lived in Edinburgh and contributed to the eighteenth-century Scottish Enlightenment. In his day, he was better known – and more widely read – as a historian than as a philosopher, having produced a six-volume history of England. In taking an empiricist approach – that all knowledge is derived from sense experience – Hume made the important distinction (which we have already discussed) between what we have called 'analytic' and 'synthetic' statements. In other words, between:

● those statements that show the relationship between ideas. These are known to be true **a priori** (before experience) because their denial involved contradiction, for instance the propositions of maths and logic. They offer certainty, but not information about the world.

and

● those that describe matters of fact. These can only be known **a posteriori** (after experience). They are not certain, but depend on empirical evidence.

This leads to what is known as Hume's Fork. In this, you may ask of a statement:

● Does it contain matters of fact? If so, relate them to experience.
● Does it give the relationships between ideas?
● If neither, then it is meaningless.

Hume's argument concerning evidence runs like this:

● I see something happen several times.
● I therefore expect it to happen again.
● I get into the mental habit of expecting it to happen.
● I may be tempted to project this mental habit out on to the external world in the form of a 'law' of physics.

So, for example, 'A causes B' could be taken to mean 'B has always been seen to follow A'.

It might be tempting to say 'Therefore B will always follow A', but this would imply that nature is uniform, and you can never have enough evidence for such an absolute statement.

To the statement 'Every event must have a cause', Hume would say:

● It can't be justified by logic, since its denial does not involve self-contradiction.
● It can't be proved from experience, because we cannot witness every event.

What, then, are we to do? Hume says that we can accept the idea of causality because it is a habit of the imagination, based on past observation. This may seem obvious, but an important distinction has been made between claiming that something *must be* the case, and saying that, in practice, we have always *found it to be* the case.

KANT

Immanuel Kant (1724–1804) is one of the most influential figures in the development of Western philosophy. His entire life was spent in Königsberg in East Prussia, where he was a professor at the university. This in itself was remarkable since, prior to the twentieth century, most philosophers were not professional academics.

In many ways, Kant's philosophy can be seen as an attempt to take seriously the claims of the empiricists (e.g. Hume) that everything depends upon experience and is open to doubt, but to do so in the context of Newtonian physics and the rise of science. Science seeks to formulate laws which predict with certainty, and causality is an essential feature of Newtonian science. We just *know* that everything will be found to have a cause, even before we experience it. So how can you reconcile an empiricist view of knowledge with common sense and the findings of science?

Kant sought to achieve this through what he called his 'Copernican Revolution'. Just as Copernicus totally changed our perception of the world by showing that the Earth revolved round the Sun and not vice versa, so Kant argued that the world of our experience is shaped by our own means of perceiving and understanding it, making the important distinction between what we perceive with our senses (which he called **phenomena**) and the world of things as they are in themselves (which he called **noumena**).

Kant argued that certain features of experience, including space, time and causality, were not in themselves features of the external world, but were imposed by the mind on experience. This was a revolutionary way of looking at the theory of knowledge and at metaphysics. Take the example of time. When I see a sequence of things, I say that time is passing and that one thing follows another. But where is that time? Is it something that exists 'out there' to be seen? Is time there to be discovered? Kant argued that time was one of the ways in which the mind organizes its experiences; it is part of our mental apparatus.

'But what happened before the "Big Bang"?' is an example of the mind trying to impose the category of time on something to which scientists try to tell us it cannot be applied. However much I accept the idea of space and time coming from that 'singularity', my mind rebels and demands yet more space and time before and beyond it. I am given a description of the universe, and ask 'But what lies outside it?' If I am told that nothing lies outside it, I become confused, for my mind automatically tries to imagine an expanse of nothingness stretching outward from what is known.

The same is true for causality. We assume that everything has a cause. Even when we have no evidence of a cause, we believe that one will be found eventually – because that is the way the world works. Kant would say that it is the way the mind works. We impose the idea of causality on our experience.

This was his way of reconciling these two important elements in the consciousness of the eighteenth century, and it has many implications for later thought.

Scepticism

The term 'sceptic' is generally used of a person who claims that we cannot know anything for certain, and that one view is likely to be as valid as any other. People tend to be sceptical about particular things – the validity of scientific claims, for example, or politics or morals.

It may be helpful, however, to make a distinction between scepticism as a conclusion and sceptical questioning as a process. Philosophers need to question and challenge all claims to knowledge, so – as a process – being sceptical about a claim is both valid and important for philosophy. However, there are some sceptical conclusions – for example, that the world as we know it may not exist at all, but may all be a dream – that are an interesting challenge, because common sense tells you that they are wrong, but the arguments for them may be difficult to refute.

THE PROOF OF THE PUDDING...

When examining matters of epistemology, you may be tempted to take a common-sense view: that a theory would seem to be right because it is the generally accepted and practical way of looking at things. We may be justified in accepting a theory if it is useful and solves problems. There is a tradition of philosophy that follows this line of reasoning: **pragmatism**. It was developed in America and is associated in particular with C.S. Peirce (1839–1914), William James (1842–1910) and John Dewey (1859–1952). In the simplest of terms, pragmatism says:

- We act; we are not just spectators. The 'facts' about the world are shaped by our concerns and what we hope to do.
- Beliefs should accord with known facts. But what should you do if the evidence is balanced between two theories?
- The answer – according to the pragmatists – is to accept the theory which gives the richer consequences; in other words, the one which will be of the greater practical use.

Dewey emphasized the fact that we are not detached observers, but that we need to survive in the world, and that *thinking is a problem-solving activity* related to that need. Science is a dynamic process of gaining knowledge, enabling us to get some mastery over our environment. Knowledge is therefore of practical importance in our lives, not simply something about which we might speculate.

SUMMARY

Today we have looked at epistemology, which is simply a smart way of saying the study of knowledge (*episteme* is the Greek word for 'knowledge'). As we have seen, epistemology asks the question: What and how do we know anything about the world? This is fundamental for any other kind of philosophical endeavour – how can we start to ask other questions, about the existence of God or the nature of the good for instance, unless we have sorted out *how* we can know anything about such things in the first place?

We have also discovered today the two broad responses that philosophers have made to the question 'How do we know?' On the one hand, rationalists from Plato onward have argued that knowledge is in some sense embedded within our minds and can be pursued by 'pure' thought or reason. On the other, empiricists, such as Aristotle, have insisted that we gain knowledge through our senses, that is, through our interaction with the world. In this debate, few thinkers have adopted

SUNDAY

MONDAY

TUESDAY

WEDNESDAY

THURSDAY

FRIDAY

SATURDAY

exclusively idealist or empirical theories of knowledge, and perhaps it is more helpful to think of these viewpoints as two ends of a continuum. Knowledge, as common sense indeed tells us, is built upon varying admixtures of both reason and sense data.

Tomorrow, Monday, we will turn to the philosophy of science.

FACT-CHECK (ANSWERS AT THE BACK)

1. According to the empiricist position, knowledge starts...
   a) In the mind ❑
   b) In the senses ❑
   c) In the external world ❑
   d) None of the above ❑

2. What is the basic idea of materialism?
   a) That what counts is material success ❑
   b) That matter is in the mind ❑
   c) That reality is what matters ❑
   d) That the ultimate reality is matter ❑

3. How might we best sum up what Descartes tried to do in his philosophy?
   a) To establish a basis for knowledge ❑
   b) To establish the self as a thinking thing ❑
   c) To doubt everything ❑
   d) All of the above ❑

4. How might we best sum up Plato's story of the cave?
   a) As a metaphor for human existence ❑
   b) As a metaphor for knowledge ❑
   c) As a metaphor for human delusion ❑
   d) None of the above ❑

5. What does Plato call the general realities that lie behind individual things?
   a) Perfections ❑
   b) Images ❑
   c) Shadows ❑
   d) Forms ❑

6. How might we best describe the philosophy of Aristotle?
   a) Idealist ❑
   b) Rationalist ❑
   c) Empiricist ❑
   d) Materialist ❑

7. Which of the following is *not* a secondary quality, according to Locke?
   a) Smell ❑
   b) Number ❑
   c) Taste ❑
   d) Sound ❑

8. 'A priori' means:
   a) Basic principle ❑
   b) First principle ❑
   c) After experience ❑
   d) Before experience ❑

9. For Hume it is impossible to justify an absolute statement because...
   a) Human perception is inherently flawed ❑
   b) Reality is always changing ❑
   c) You can never have enough evidence ❑
   d) None of the above ❑

10. Which of the following are examples of Kantian noumena?
    a) Higgs boson particle ❑
    b) A table ❑
    c) A newly discovered planet ❑
    d) All and none of the above ❑

MONDAY

The philosophy of science

The philosophy of science examines the methods used by science, the ways in which hypotheses and laws are formulated from evidence, and the grounds on which scientific claims about the world may be justified.

Today we take a brief look at the historical development of the relationship between philosophy and science from ancient Greek thought, through the Newtonian world, to the impact of relativity and quantum mechanics in the twentieth century. We shall see that individual sciences have moved away from being 'natural philosophy' and philosophy has taken on a positive but critical role with respect to the way in which science presents its findings.

We then examine the 'inductive' method by which science moves from evidence to theory, the way in which theories may be falsified, the problems associated with holding apparently incompatible but equally valid theories, and the way in which authority is exercised within the scientific community.

THE DEVELOPMENT OF SCIENCE

Within Western thought there have been two major shifts in the view of the world, and these have had an important influence on the way in which philosophy and science have related to one another. We may therefore divide Western philosophy of science into three general periods: early Greek and medieval thought; the Newtonian world-view; and twentieth-century developments (although recognizing that such division represents a simplification of a more complex process of change).

EARLY GREEK AND MEDIEVAL THOUGHT

In 529 CE the Emperor Justinian banned the teaching of philosophy in order to further the interests of Christianity. Plato had already had a considerable influence upon the development of Christian doctrines, and elements of his thought – particularly the contrast between the ideal world of the Forms and the limited world of everyday experience – continued within theology. The works of Aristotle were preserved first in Byzantium and then by the Arabs, being rediscovered in the thirteenth century, when the first translations were made from Arabic into Latin.

In the thirteenth century, with thinkers like Thomas Aquinas (1225–74), Duns Scotus (1266–1308) and William of Ockham (c.1285–1349), Greek thought began to be explored again in a systematic way. From that time, philosophy is very much a development of, or reaction to, the work of the Greeks.

For Plato, the unseen 'Forms' were more real than the individual things that could be known through the senses. This way of thinking (backed by religion) suggested that human reason and its concepts of perfection were paramount, and that observation and experience were secondary.

Cosmology and astronomy give examples of this trend: Copernicus (1473–1543) and later Galileo (1564–1642) were to offer a view of the universe in which the Earth revolved around the Sun, rather than vice versa. Their view was opposed by those whose idea of the universe came from Ptolemy and in which the Earth was surrounded by glassy spheres – perfect shapes, conveying the Sun, Moon and planets in perfect circular motion. Their work was challenged (and Galileo condemned) not because their observations were found to be at fault, but because they had trusted their observations, rather than deciding beforehand what should be the case. From his observations Kepler (1571–1630) controversially concluded that the orbit of Mars was elliptical, whereas all heavenly motion was thought to be perfect, and therefore circular.

These astronomers were struggling against a background of religious authority which gave Greek notions of perfection priority over observations and experimental evidence. In other words, the earlier medieval system of thought was deductive (it deduced what should be observed to happen from its preconceived ideas), in contrast to the later inductive method of developing a theory from observations.

Along with the tendency to look for theory and perfection rather than accept the results of observation, there was another, stemming from Aristotle. Following his idea of the final cause, everything was thought to be designed for a particular purpose. If something falls to the ground, it seeks its natural purpose and place in doing so. So, in a religious context, it was possible to say that something happened because it was God's will for it, or because it was designed for that purpose.

THE NEWTONIAN WORLD-VIEW

The rise of modern science would not have been possible without the renewed sense of the value of human reason and the ability to challenge established ideas and religious dogma, which developed as a result of the Renaissance and the Reformation. But what was equally influential was the way in which information was gathered and sorted, and theories formed on the basis of it. Central to this process was the method of induction, and this was set out very clearly (and in a way that continues to be relevant) by Francis Bacon.

Bacon (1561–1626) rejected Aristotle's idea of final causes, and insisted that knowledge should be based on a process of induction, which, as we shall see later, is the systematic method of coming to general conclusions on the basis of evidence about individual instances that have been observed. He warned about 'idols' that tend to lead a person astray:

- the desire to accept that which confirms what we already believe
- distortions resulting from our habitual ways of thinking
- muddles that come through our use of language (e.g. using the same word for different things, and then assuming that they must be one and the same)
- believing things out of allegiance to a particular school of thought.

Bacon also pointed out that, in gathering evidence, one should not just look for examples that confirm a particular theory, but one should actively seek out and accept the force of contrary examples. After centuries of using evidence to confirm what was already known by dogma or reason, this was quite revolutionary.

With Bacon and Newton, science became about gathering evidence.

The general view of the world which came about as a result of the rise of science is usually linked with the name of Isaac Newton (1642–1727). In the Newtonian world-view, observation and experiment yield knowledge of the laws which govern the world.

In it, space and time were fixed, forming a framework within which everything takes place. Objects were seen to move and be moved through the operation of physical laws of motion, so that everything was seen as a machine, the workings of which could become known through careful observation. Interlocking forces kept matter in motion, and everything was predictable. Not everything might be known at this moment, but there was no doubt that everything would be understood eventually, using the established scientific method.

With the coming of the Newtonian world-view, the function of philosophy changed. Rather than initiating theories about cosmology, the task of philosophy was to examine and comment on the methods and results of scientific method, establishing its limits. Kant, for example, argued that space, time and causality – the very bases of Newtonian science – were not to be found 'out there' in the world of independent objects, but were contributed by the mind. We see things as being in space and time because that is the way our minds process the information given through the senses.

Hume pointed out that scientific laws were not true universal statements, but only summaries of what had been experienced so far. The method used by science – gathering data and drawing general conclusions from it – yielded higher and higher degrees of probability, but could never achieve absolute certainty.

TWENTIETH-CENTURY DEVELOPMENTS

For most thinkers prior to the twentieth century, it was inconceivable that space and time were not fixed: a necessary framework within which everything else could take place.

Einstein's theories of relativity were to change all that. The first, in 1905, was the theory of *Special Relativity*, best known in the form of the equation $E = mc^2$. This showed that mass and energy are equivalent, and that (since energy was equal to mass multiplied by the speed of light squared) a very small amount of matter could be converted into a very large amount of energy. This, of course, is now best known for its rather drastic practical consequences in the development of nuclear weapons.

Einstein published the second theory, *General Relativity*, in 1916. It made the revolutionary claim that time, space, matter and energy were all related to one another. For example, space and time can be compressed by a strong gravitational field. There are no fixed points. The way in which things relate to one another depends upon the point from which they are being observed.

Alongside relativity came quantum mechanics, which raised questions about whether events at the subatomic level could be predicted, and what it means to say that one thing causes another. Quantum mechanics is notoriously difficult to understand. A general view of it is that it works, so there must be something right about it, even if we don't understand it as a theory. What is certain is that quantum mechanics, however little understood, when combined with the theories of relativity, rendered the old Newtonian certainties obsolete. Newton's laws of physics might still apply, but only within very limited parameters. Once you stray into the microscopic area of the subatomic, or the macroscopic world of cosmic structures, the situation is quite different.

In the twentieth century, therefore, philosophy engaged with a scientific view of the world that had changed enormously from the mechanical and predictable world of Newton. In particular, science started to offer a variety of ways of picturing the world, and cosmology – which had been dominated first by religious belief and Aristotle, and then by astronomy – was now very much in the hands of mathematicians. It became clear that the world as a whole was not something that could be observed; its structures could only be explored by calculation.

During much of the first half of the twentieth century, philosophy (at least in the United States and Britain) became dominated by the quest for meaning and the analysis of language. It no longer saw its role as providing an overview

Since Einstein, scientific method has shifted decisively towards the rational world of mathematics.

of the universe – it left that to the individual scientific disciplines. Rather, it adopted a supportive role, checking on the methods used by science, the logic by which results were produced from observations, and the way in which theories could be confirmed or discredited.

FROM EVIDENCE TO THEORY: SCIENTIFIC METHOD

In terms of the philosophy of science, the most important approach to gathering and analysing information was the 'inductive method'. This was championed by Francis Bacon, and then by Thomas Hobbes (1588–1679), and became the

SUNDAY

MONDAY

TUESDAY

WEDNESDAY

THURSDAY

FRIDAY

SATURDAY

basis of the Newtonian world of science. In its practical approach to sifting and evaluating evidence, it is also reflected in the empiricism of Hume. Indeed, it was the inductive method that distinguished 'modern' science from what had gone before, and brought in the first of the two major shifts in world-view.

THE INDUCTIVE METHOD

This method is based on two things:

1 The trust that knowledge can be gained by gathering evidence and conducting experiments, i.e. it is based on facts that can be checked, or on experiments that can be repeated.
2 The willingness to set aside preconceived views about the likely outcome of an experiment, or the validity of evidence presented, i.e. the person using this method does not have a fixed idea about its conclusion, but is prepared to examine both results and methods used with an open mind.

With the inductive method, science was claiming to be based on objectively considered evidence, and was therefore seen as in contrast to traditional religion and metaphysics, which were seen to be based on doctrines that a person was required to accept and which were backed up by authority rather than reason alone.

In practice, the method works in this way:

1 Observe and gather data (evidence, information), seeking to eliminate, as far as possible, all irrelevant factors.
2 Analyse your data, and draw conclusions from them in the form of hypotheses.
3 Devise experiments to test out those hypotheses, i.e. if this hypothesis is correct, then certain experimental results should be anticipated.
4 Modify your hypothesis, if necessary, in the light of the results of your experiments.
5 From the experiments, the data and the hypotheses, argue for a theory.
6 Once you have a theory, you can predict other things on the basis of it, by which the theory can later be verified or falsified.

It is clear that this process of induction, by which a theory is arrived at by the analysis and testing out of observed data, can yield at most only a high degree of probability. There is always the chance that an additional piece of information will show that the original hypothesis is wrong, or that it applies only within a limited field. The hypothesis, and the scientific theory that comes from it, is therefore open to modification.

Scientific laws

Theories that are tested out in this way lead to the framing of scientific laws. Now it is important to establish exactly what is meant by 'law' in this context. In common parlance, 'law' is taken to be something which is imposed, a rule that is to be obeyed. But it would be wrong to assume that a scientific law can dictate how things behave. The law simply describes that behaviour; it does not control it (as Hume argued). If something behaves differently, it is not to be blamed for going against a law of nature. It is simply that either:

- there is an unknown factor that has influenced this particular situation and therefore modified what was expected, or
- the law of nature is inadequately framed, and needs to be modified in order to take this new situation into account.

FALSIFICATION

It may sound illogical, but science makes progress when a theory is falsified, rather than when it is confirmed, for it is only by rejecting and modifying a theory, to account for new evidence, that something better is put in its place. This view was argued very effectively by Karl Popper (1902–94), an Austrian philosopher from Vienna, who moved to New Zealand in 1937 and then to London in 1945, where he became Professor of Logic and Scientific Method at the London School of Economics. He was a socialist and made significant contributions to political philosophy as well as the philosophy of science.

In his book *The Logic of Scientific Discovery* (1934; translated in 1959) Popper makes the crucial point that science seeks theories that are logically self-consistent, and that can be falsified. He points out that a scientific law goes beyond what can be experienced. We can never prove it to be absolutely true; all we can do is try to prove it to be false, and accept it on a provisional basis until such time as it is falsified.

This leads Popper to say that a scientific theory cannot be compatible with all the logically possible evidence that could be considered. It must be possible to falsify it. If a theory claims that it can never be falsified, then it is not scientific. On this basis, he challenged the ideas of both Marx and Freud.

Where you have a choice of theories, Popper held that you should accept the one that is not only better corroborated, but also more testable and entailing more true statements than the others. And that you should do this, even if you know that the theory is false. Since we cannot, anyway, have absolute certainty, we have to go for the most useful way of understanding the world that we have to hand, even if its limitations have already been revealed.

RIGHT, WRONG OR WHAT?

As laws and theories become established within the scientific community, they are used as a basis for further research, and are termed 'paradigms'. Occasionally there is a paradigm shift, which entails the revision of much of science. In terms of cosmology, the move from an Aristotelian (Ptolemaic) to a Newtonian world-view, and then the further move from that to the view of Einstein, represents two shifts of paradigm.

T.S. Kuhn, in his book *The Structure of Scientific Revolutions* (1962), described these paradigms as the basic Gestalt (or world-view) within which science at any one time interprets the evidence it has available. It is the paradigm that largely dictates scientific progress, and observations are not free from the influence of the paradigm either.

What makes Kuhn's theory particularly controversial is that he claims that there is no *independent* data by which to decide between competing paradigms (since all data is presented either in terms of one paradigm or the other) and therefore there is no strictly logical reason to change a paradigm. This implies a relativism in science, which seemed to threaten the logical basis of the development of scientific theories, as expounded by Karl Popper.

The general implication of the work of Kuhn and others is that, if a theory works well (in other words, if it gives good predictive results), then it becomes a *possible* explanation: we cannot say that it is *the definitive or only one*.

WHAT COUNTS AS SCIENCE?

At one time, an activity could be called 'scientific' if it followed the inductive method. On these grounds, the work of Marx could be called scientific, in that he based his theories on accounts of political changes in the societies he studied. Similarly, behavioural psychology can claim to be scientific on the basis of the methods used: observing and recording the responses of people and animals to particular stimuli, for example. So science is generally defined by method rather than by subject.

Popper criticized both Marx and Freud, not because he considered they failed to observe and gather evidence, but because of what he saw as their willingness to interpret new evidence in the light of their theories, rather than to allow that evidence to challenge or modify those theories. So how should we distinguish between science and what Popper called 'pseudo-science'?

Distinguishing features of science include the consistent attempt at the disinterested gathering of information and the willingness to accept revisions of one's theories.

FOR REFLECTION

Science offers a very rich and exciting view of the world. Whether you start by considering the idea that matter is a collection of nuclear forces, rather than something solid and tangible, or whether you start with the idea that the universe is expanding outwards from the space-time singularity, creating its own space and time as it does so, modern science seems to contradict our common-sense notions. Yet, in doing so, it performs the valuable function of shaking us out of our ordinary assumptions and reminding us that the world is not as simple as may at first sight appear. In this, science acts rather like philosophy: challenging our assumptions and examining the basis of what we can say about reality.

SUMMARY

In today's chapter we have probed the evolving relationship of philosophy and science from ancient to modern times and, with the Newtonian revolution, the development of a philosophy *of* science. It may be useful to sum up here what exactly is encompassed by this branch of philosophy and what is not:

- Philosophy cannot determine what information is available to science: it cannot provide data.
- Philosophy examines the use of scientific data, and the logical processes by which this information can become the basis of scientific theories.
- Most importantly, philosophy can remind scientists that facts always contain an element of interpretation. Facts are the product of a thinking mind encountering external evidence, and they therefore contain both that evidence and the mental framework by means of which it has been apprehended, and through which it is articulated.

SUNDAY

MONDAY

TUESDAY

WEDNESDAY

THURSDAY

FRIDAY

SATURDAY

FACT-CHECK (ANSWERS AT THE BACK)

1. Medieval science and philosophy were dominated by...
   a) Theory ❏
   b) Religion ❏
   c) Greek thought ❏
   d) All of the above ❏

2. Following Aristotle's idea of a final cause, everything...
   a) Has its origins in a deity ❏
   b) Has an observable cause ❏
   c) Was designed with a purpose ❏
   d) None of the above ❏

3. The role of philosophy in medieval times was to...
   a) Show that reason could confirm traditional ideas ❏
   b) Come up with theories ❏
   c) To examine scientific methods ❏
   d) All of the above ❏

4. Which of the following hindered science, according to Francis Bacon?
   a) Habitual ways of thinking ❏
   b) Imprecise use of language ❏
   c) Looking only for evidence that confirms pre-existing ideas ❏
   d) All of the above ❏

5. By the time of Newton, the role of philosophy was to...
   a) Challenge evidence ❏
   b) Initiate theories ❏
   c) Examine the methods used in science ❏
   d) Provide an alternative to science ❏

6. According to Hume, scientific theories are...
   a) Universal ❏
   b) Temporary ❏
   c) Absolute ❏
   d) Probable ❏

7. From the twentieth century, our view of the cosmos was increasingly...
   a) Mathematical ❏
   b) Observable ❏
   c) Predictable ❏
   d) Mechanical ❏

8. Put the following stages in the inductive method of doing science in order:
   a) The development of a theory ❏
   b) The testing of a hypothesis ❏
   c) The observation of data ❏
   d) The analysis of data ❏

9. Popper defined a scientific theory as one that is...
   a) Verifiable ❏
   b) Falsifiable ❏
   c) Provable ❏
   d) Unchallengeable ❏

10. Kuhn argued that a scientific theory works well if...
    a) It is absolutely correct ❏
    b) It enables good predictions ❏
    c) It does not require evidence ❏
    d) It excludes alternatives ❏

TUESDAY

Language and logic

Philosophy depends on language, so understanding the nature and function of language is key to unpicking philosophical problems. Early in the twentieth century some philosophers argued that statements could be meaningful only if they could be backed up by empirical evidence, leading to the radical conclusion that metaphysics, theology, ethics and aesthetics were all factually meaningless and merely reflected personal wishes and opinions.

Later, particularly as a result of the work of Wittgenstein, language was seen as performing a variety of different functions. Rather than attempting to understand the truth of a statement in terms of factual evidence, its meaning became known through the function it performed and the 'language game' within which it was played.

Today's chapter will also look at linguistic philosophy, an approach which argues that philosophical problems can be solved by clarifying the ordinary language that people use, and also at formal logic, which analyses arguments using shorthand notation.

The language we use colours the way in which we think and experience the world.

It is therefore most unwise to philosophize without being aware of the role played by language. In looking at language, however, there are three quite different things to examine:

1 the **philosophy of language** (which looks at what language is, how it works, whether statements are meaningful and how it may be verified)
2 **linguistic philosophy** (which is a way of doing philosophy through the analysis of problematic statements)
3 **logic** (which examines the structure of arguments, in order to illustrate whether their conclusions can be shown to follow from their premises).

LANGUAGE AND CERTAINTY

A key question for the study of language is **verification**. How can you show that a statement is true?

● Do you set out bits of evidence that correspond to each of the words used? (An empiricist might encourage you to do that. A reductionist might say that your statement was nonsense unless you could do it!) This assumes that language has a picturing or pointing function.
● Is a statement 'true' if its logic is sound? If so, does its truth also depend on some sort of external evidence?

The distinction between 'synthetic' and 'analytic' statements has already been made. But language is complex: an average line of poetry, a joke, a command, a piece of moral advice or the whispered endearments of lovers can quickly dispel any simple theory of verification. We need to move on from 'Is it true?' to the broader issue of 'What, if anything, does it mean?'.

Probably the greatest influence in shaping modern life is science, which (as we saw on Monday) is based on observation of the world, and uses empirical data to form hypotheses. With the obvious success of science, it was very tempting for philosophers to see science as in some way a paradigm for the way in which knowledge as a whole could be gained.

'Whereof one cannot speak, thereof one must be silent.'

As science is based on observation, each claim it makes is backed up with reference to data of some sort. Without data, there is no science. The language used by science is therefore justified with reference to external objects. It 'pictures' them. A statement is true if it corresponds to what has been observed, false if it does not so correspond. But can this test be applied to all language?

LOGICAL POSITIVISM

Ludwig Wittgenstein (1889–1951), an Austrian who did most of his philosophy in Cambridge and studied under Bertrand Russell, was deeply impressed by the work done in mathematics and logic by Gottlob Frege (1848–1925), Russell and A.N. Whitehead, with whom Russell had written *Principia*

Mathematica, a major work attempting to establish the logical foundations of mathematics. These thinkers had argued that logic and mathematics were objective, not subjective; that is, they described features of the external world, rather than simply showing ways in which the mind worked.

Wittgenstein suggested that philosophical problems would be solved if the language people used corresponded to the phenomenal world, both in terms of logic and the evidence for what was being said. In the opening statement of his hugely influential book *Tractatus Logico-Philosophicus* (1921), he identifies the world with the sum of true propositions: 'The world is all that is the case', but he has to acknowledge that there are therefore certain things of which one cannot speak. One of these is the subject self: 'The subject does not belong to the world; rather it is a limit of the world.' Another is the mystical sense of the world as a whole. Whatever cannot be shown to correspond to some observable reality, cannot be meaningfully spoken about.

His ideas were taken up by the Vienna Circle, a group of philosophers who met in that city during the 1920s and 1930s. The approach they took is generally known as **logical positivism**. Broadly, logical positivism claims that:

- Analytic propositions tell us nothing about the world. They are true by definition, and therefore tautologies. They include the statements of logic and mathematics.
- Synthetic propositions depend on evidence. Therefore there can be no necessary synthetic propositions.
- Metaphysics and theology are literally 'meaningless' – since such statements are neither matters of logic (and therefore true by definition – a priori) nor are they provable by empirical evidence.

Moritz Schlick, one of the Vienna Circle, argued that 'the meaning of a statement is its method of verification'. This became known as the 'Verification Principle'.

Logical positivism was promoted by the British philosopher A.J. Ayer (1910–89) in an important book entitled *Language, Truth and Logic* (1936). In that book he asks: 'What can philosophy do?' His answer is that it certainly cannot tell us the nature of reality as such – in other words, it cannot provide us with metaphysics. If we want to know about reality, we have to rely upon the evidence of our senses.

He therefore argued that philosophy cannot actually give new information about anything, but has the task of analysis and clarification. It looks at the words people use and analyses them, showing their logical implications. By doing so, philosophy clarifies otherwise muddled thought.

Statements are meaningless if there is nothing that would count for or against them being true. On this basis, much of what passes for religious language, or aesthetics, or morality, would be categorized as 'meaningless', because none of these things can be specified in terms of concrete facts that can be checked by observation.

The key thing about logical positivism was that it represented a particularly strong form of empiricism and a particularly narrow form of language. The service it rendered philosophy was that, by arguing that a wide range of propositions were 'meaningless', it forced philosophers to think again about the way in which we use language. Whereas the logical positivists had concentrated on a simple 'picturing' view of language, it was soon realized that language can be meaningful in terms of many other functions (for example: expressing feelings; giving commands; stating preferences). In this way, by reacting against the logical positivists, it became widely recognized that a more sophistical view of the function of language needed to be developed.

KNOWLEDGE AND LANGUAGE

As far as philosophers in the Anglo-American tradition were concerned, for much of the twentieth century philosophy was dominated by the discussion of language. Indeed, there was a feeling that this was all that philosophy was about – everything else being sorted out by sciences or politics or sociology. Philosophy, rather than having any specific content, was an activity, and that activity was to do with the sorting out of words and their meaning. So philosophy was given a role rather like that of an indigestion tablet, something necessary in order to purify the system and enable comfort and efficiency to return. *Philosophy, according to that view, would help every other subject by clearing away its linguistic confusions.*

'I said, clearer, not louder!'

Early in the twentieth century, as we previously saw, the logical positivists argued that the meaning of a statement was its method of verification. This view attempted to purge language of all that could not be reduced to sense experience. Metaphysics was out, and ethics was little more than the expression of a preference.

By the 1950s this view of language was becoming broader. Wittgenstein (who, in the earlier phase of his work, had espoused this radically reductionist approach to language) broadened his view, and accepted that language could take on different functions, of which straight description of phenomena was only one. This allowed greater flexibility, and recognized that the expression of values and emotions, the giving of orders and making of requests, were all valid uses of language. His keynote was that language was a 'form of life' and that, to understand it, it had to be observed in use.

He described the different uses of language as 'language games'. Just as a game, such as chess, can be appreciated only once the rules for moving the various pieces are understood, so language can be understood only within its context; words have meaning that is related to their function in the 'game'. This is not to trivialize language (it is not a 'game' in that sense), but to recognize that language is a tool for doing something – a tool that is based on rules that are understood by those who use it.

At this point, philosophers seemed to be catching up with common sense, and abandoning the purity of the unchallengeable statement as the goal of meaning. To know the meaning of a statement, you have to see it in its context and understand what it is intended to achieve. On Friday we shall be examining different tasks that language can perform in the field of ethics. What we need to recognize at this point is that language is neither simple nor transparent.

LINGUISTIC PHILOSOPHY

While the logical positivists were analysing statements in terms of their verification through sense experience, other philosophers – notably, G.E. Moore (1873–1958) and J.L. Austin (1911–60) – were investigating the ordinary use of words. Along with the broader approach taken by Wittgenstein, this led to the view that ordinary speech was an activity that could be analysed to show its internal logic and implications, and that such analysis would clarify meanings and therefore solve philosophical problems.

This approach, known as 'linguistic philosophy', became a dominant feature of philosophy in the 1940s and 1950s. On Wednesday we shall see that one of the most controversial books on the philosophy of mind at the time was entitled *The Concept of Mind*, and offered a radical view of mind based on the analysis of ordinary language.

And here is the key to what linguistic philosophy was about: it worked on the assumption that philosophical problems came about because of the ambiguities and confusions of normal speech. Once that speech could be analysed and its confusions exposed, new insights and clarity would emerge.

FORMAL LOGIC

Logic is the branch of philosophy that examines the process of reasoning. When you start with a set of premises and reach a conclusion from them, the process of doing so is called **deductive logic**. An argument is *valid* if it is impossible for the conclusions to be false if the premises are true. An argument can be valid even if the premises are false (and therefore the conclusion is false); just because you are mistaken, it does not mean that your reasoning is not logical. An argument where the premises are true and the logic is valid is *sound*.

Logic has a long history. In Plato's dialogues we find Socrates debating with various people. He invites them to put forward propositions and then analyses their implications and the arguments they have used. His argument often takes the form of, 'If B follows from A, and B is clearly wrong, then A must also have been wrong.'

But the main influence on logic for two thousand years was Aristotle. He set down the basic features of deductive logic, in particular the **syllogism**, in which major and minor premises lead to a conclusion.

The most quoted piece of logic ever has to be the syllogism:

All men are mortal.
Socrates is a man.
Therefore Socrates is mortal.

This can be expressed as:

All As are B.
C is an A.
Therefore C is B.

From the basic syllogism, we can go on to explore the forms of **inference** – in other words, what can validly follow from what.

Some principles of logic appear quite obvious, but are crucially important for clarifying arguments. William of

Ockham (1285–1349), a logician who commented on Aristotle, is best known for his argument that one should not multiply entities unnecessarily. In other words, given a number of possible explanations, one should incline towards the simplest. This is generally known as Ockham's Razor.

Logic is often able to highlight common errors. One of these is known as the *argumentum ad ignorantiam*, which is to argue for something on the grounds that there is no evidence against it, whereas to establish that something is the case, one needs to show evidence for it.

Logic can become very complex, with parts of an argument depending on others: 'if not this, then that, but if that then something else...'. Clearly, it would be cumbersome to write out all the elements of each argument in order to examine the logic involved.

To overcome this problem, formal logic uses an artificial form of language. This language uses sets of letters, A, B, C, etc., to stand for the various component premises and conclusions, and also a set of signs to act as connectives. These signs stand for such logical steps as 'and', 'or', 'it is not the case that', 'if ... then' and 'if and only if'.

This use of artificial languages is particularly associated with the German philosopher and mathematician Gottlob Frege (1848–1925).

Example

The connective 'if ... then' is shown by an arrow pointing to the right. The conclusion (therefore) is shown as a semicolon.

Take this argument:

I have missed the train. If I miss the train, I arrive late at work. Therefore I shall arrive late at work.

We can formalize this by using the letter 'A' for 'I have missed the train' and 'B' for 'I will arrive late at work'.

Rewritten, the argument becomes:

$$A \, (A \rightarrow B); B$$

An important feature of logic is that it breaks down each sentence into its component parts and makes clear the relationship between them. So formal logic helps to clarify exactly what is and what is not valid. Arguments set out in this way can become very complex indeed, and there are a large number of unfamiliar signs used for the various connectives. If you pick up a copy of Russell and Whitehead's famous *Principia Mathematica* or browse through *The Journal of Symbolic Logic*, you will see page after page of what looks like advanced mathematics or complex scientific formulae. For the uninitiated, it is extremely difficult to follow!

SUMMARY

Today we have broached the tricky subject of the relationship between philosophy and language, which, in the twentieth century, moved centre stage. Let's try to summarize, in simple terms, what we have learned:

People (hopefully) think before they speak. They may also perceive before they think.

Therefore, what they say reflects the nature of thought and of perception. Language is therefore only as simple and straightforward as the thought and perception that produced it.

Add intuition, emotion, existential angst and the general confusions of human life, and the resulting language is very complex indeed. It may perform many different functions. It may play many different games.

We may not even be aware of the implications of what we are saying, which is to return to Plato, who in his dialogues portrays Socrates as a man who is constantly asking people what they mean, and thereby exposing their confusions and opening up the way to greater clarity.

SUNDAY

MONDAY

TUESDAY

WEDNESDAY

THURSDAY

FRIDAY

SATURDAY

Without language we cannot have metaphysics or epistemology: indeed, we cannot have philosophy, civilization, culture or other distinctively human features of life.

FACT-CHECK (ANSWERS AT THE BACK)

1. What is the name of Wittgenstein's ground-breaking 1921 work?
a) *Principia Mathematica* ❑
b) *Tractatus Logico-Philosophicus* ❑
c) *Philosophical Investigations* ❑
d) *Language, Truth and Knowledge* ❑

2. According to the logical positivists, metaphysics is...
a) Meaningless ❑
b) Empirically unprovable ❑
c) Not a matter of logic ❑
d) All of the above ❑

3. What, according to Ayer, is the role of philosophy?
a) To discover new information about the world ❑
b) To analyse language ❑
c) To clarify thought ❑
d) None of the above ❑

4. Which of the following sum up the position of logical positivism?
a) A renewed emphasis on metaphysics ❑
b) Mistrust of the traditional language of philosophy ❑
c) A preference for scientific language ❑
d) A strong empiricism ❑

5. Who described the different uses of language as 'language games'?
a) Ayer ❑
b) Russell ❑
c) Wittgenstein ❑
d) Schlick ❑

6. What is linguistic philosophy?
a) The use of philosophy to solve linguistic problems ❑
b) The use of everyday language to analyse philosophical problems ❑
c) The analysis of language to solve philosophical problems ❑
d) None of the above ❑

7. Which of the following are notable linguistic philosophers?
a) Ayer ❑
b) Moore ❑
c) Austin ❑
d) Russell ❑

8. What is logic? The branch of philosophy that examines...
a) Philosophical statements ❑
b) The process of reasoning ❑
c) The validity of premises ❑
d) None of the above ❑

9. A classic (categorical) syllogism consists of how many parts?
a) Two ❑
b) Three. ❑
c) Four ❑
d) As many as you like ❑

10. What is Ockham's Razor?
a) A way of reducing complex arguments down to their simplest form ❑
b) A new kind of facial hair remover ❑
c) The idea that the simplest explanation is probably the best ❑
d) The use of rapier-like logic to destroy an opponent's argument ❑

WEDNESDAY

The philosophy of mind

The philosophy of mind explores what we mean by the 'mind' and how it relates to the body. Some argue for materialism – that what we experience as mind is no more than brain activity or a description of physical activity. Other thinkers opt for some kind of dualism, in which the mind is distinct from the body although causally linked to it. Any theory needs to take into account the experienced fact that minds and bodies interact.

We shall then look briefly at the question of whether it is possible for a computer to reproduce what we mean by mind, before moving on to questions about personal freedom, identity and how we can know and relate to other people.

Today the traditional discussions in the philosophy of mind are set in the broad context of the cognitive sciences – including neuroscience, pharmacology and the creation of artificial intelligence – but the question remains how these branches of science relate to our experience of ourselves as thinking, feeling individuals.

THE REAL YOU?

As you read this book, your eyes are scanning from left to right, your fingers turn the pages, your brain is consuming energy, taking oxygen from its blood supply, tiny electrical impulses are passing between brain cells. All that is part of the physical world, and can be detected scientifically. How does all that relate to the process of reading, thinking, learning and remembering? And how do both relate to personal identity?

If, as the result of an accident, I were to have an arm or leg amputated, I should refer to the detached member as 'my arm' or 'my leg', not in the sense that I owned it, but that I regarded it as part of myself, a part which I must now do without. In the same way, I can list all the parts of myself: my hair, my face, my body, my mind, my emotions, my attitudes. Some of these will be parts of my mental make-up; others will be parts of my physical body.

Where in all this is the real 'me'?

● Am I to be identified with my physical body?
● Am I my mind?
● Could I exist outside my body?
● If so, could I continue to exist after the death of my body?
● Is my mind the same thing as my brain?
● If not, then where is my mind?
● Can I ever really know other people's minds, or do I just look, listen and guess what they're thinking?
● What about computer-created artificial intelligence?

These are just some of the questions that are explored within the philosophy of mind. Its issues relate to biology, psychology, sociology, computer science, and all aspects of human thought, memory, communication and personal identity.

SUNDAY
MONDAY
TUESDAY
WEDNESDAY
THURSDAY
FRIDAY
SATURDAY

'I think, therefore I am'

In looking at the theory of knowledge, we found that Descartes – using the method of systematic doubt in his quest for certainty – could doubt everything except his own existence as a thinking being. Hence his key statement: 'I think, therefore I am.' This provided him with a starting point from which to build up knowledge. But it also created an absolute distinction between the physical body (which is extended in time and space and which can be known to the senses), and the mind (which is not extended, and which has one function – to think).

So, while Plato can speak of a physical body, with an animating self, ruled by a thinking self, and while Aristotle sees the self as that which gives form and purpose to the physical body, Descartes absolutely pulls apart the physical and the mental – the one is in the world of space and time; the other is not.

Cogito ergo sum!

THE RELATIONSHIP BETWEEN MIND AND BODY

Philosophy has explored a whole range of possible relationships between mind and body. At one extreme there is the view that what we call 'mind' is simply a way of describing the physical body and its activities (**materialism** and **behaviourism**); at the other is the rarer idea that everything is fundamentally mental (**idealism**). Between these is the view that both bodies and minds have distinct but related realities (**dualism**).

MATERIALISM

A materialist attempts to explain everything in terms of physical objects, and tends to deny the reality of anything that cannot be reduced to them. So, for a materialist, the mind or 'self' is nothing more than a way of describing physical bodies and their activity. We may experience something as a thought or an emotion, but in fact it is *nothing but* the electrical impulses in the brain, or chemical or other reactions in the rest of the body.

IDEALISM

A criticism of the idealist approach might be that, although we may not be certain of the existence of matter, for all practical purposes we have to assume it. However much our knowledge of other people is the result of our interpretation of the sense impressions we receive, we are forced by common sense to infer that there really are people with minds and bodies like our own. One of the key problems of a strictly idealist approach is that it leads to **solipsism** – the view that we are unable to know other minds, forever locked in the lonely contemplation of our own sense experience. Perhaps understandably, idealism has not been a popular approach to the issue of how mind and body are related.

DUALISM

If neither the materialist nor the idealist position convinces you by its account for the relationship between mind and body, the answer may be sought in some form of dualism: that mind and body are distinct and very different things. Each is seen as part of the self, part of what it means to be a person, but the question then becomes: How do these two things interact?

One danger here is to imagine the mind as some kind of subtle, invisible body, existing in the world of space and time, yet not subject to its usual rules of cause and effect. This, of course, is a rather crude caricature of what Descartes and other dualists have actually claimed.

THE CONCEPT OF MIND

Gilbert Ryle suggested, in *The Concept of Mind* (1949), that to speak of minds and bodies as though they were equivalent things was a **category mistake**. To explain what he meant by this he used the example of someone visiting a university and seeing many different colleges, libraries and research laboratories. The visitor then asks, 'But where is the University?' The answer, of course, is that there is no university over and above all its component parts that have already been visited. The term 'university' is a way of describing all of these things together – it is a term from another category, not the same category as the individual components.

In the same way, Ryle argued that you should not expect to find a 'mind' over and above all the various parts of the body and its actions, for 'mind' is a term from another category, a way of describing bodies and the way in which they operate.

If I say that someone is 'irritable', I do not mean that I have some privileged access to an 'irritability factor' in their mind. I just mean that, given a situation that is not to his or her liking, he or she is likely to start complaining, sulking, etc. In other words, the irritability is simply a way of describing a disposition.

Thus, for Ryle, the ascription of mental predicates (clever etc.) does not require the existence of a separate, invisible thing called a mind. The description 'clever' may indeed refer to the way in which something is done, but, equally, cleverness cannot be defined simply in terms of that action. What is clever for one person might not be so for another, and the mental description refers more to the way in which the individual person habitually relates to the world, and the expectation a person would have of him or her, rather than some special quality of an action that makes it clever.

One particular difficulty with identifying a mental phenomena with physical actions is illustrated by the idea of pain:

- I may shout, cry, hold the afflicted part of my body; I may scream and roll on the ground, curl up, look ashen. But none of these things is actually the same thing as the pain I am experiencing. The pain is indicated by them, but not defined by them.
- I may watch an actor performing all the things listed above. But, because he or she is acting, I do not imagine that there is any actual pain.
- Yet, if being in pain is actually identified with those things (as Ryle implies), then the actor is in pain.

Much modern debate on the mind/body issue has been prompted by Ryle's critique of dualism. One feature of his work that one should keep in mind is that his approach is linguistic. He asks what it means to ascribe mental predicates. The question remains, of this or any similar approach, whether the meaning of the mental predicate is the same as its method of verification. I can verify my description of someone as clever by observing and listening to him or her. But is the information I receive in that way identical to what I mean by cleverness? Or is cleverness hinted at by, but not defined by, such information?

The real threat of Ryle's argument to those who wish to maintain the idea of an independent, separate 'soul' over and above the body, is that he shows that most of what we say about people and their personalities can be justified with reference to their words, actions and general dispositions. Hence, in ordinary discussion about people, the idea of a separate soul is redundant.

A 'PLACE' FOR MIND?

A basic question for mind/body, as for many other areas of philosophy is: Can something exist if it does not have a place within the world of space and time?

It is clear, for example, following Ryle, that there is no place for a 'self' or 'soul' alongside the body. Everything to which language about the mind refers has its own place in the world – the clever action, the kindly word – and he is surely right to claim that the words 'clever' and 'kindly' here would not refer to some occult substance, but to the way in which particular deeds are performed.

But the dualist is not actually saying that the mind exists physically outside the body. The dualist position is that the mind is not extended, that it does not exist within time and space. We have returned therefore to the fundamental philosophical issue of reductionism. Consider any piece of music:

- It comprises a sequence of sound waves within the air.
- There is no music apart from those sound waves. For even if I have a tune running in my head (a problematic thing for any philosopher to say), what I am doing is recalling that pattern of sound waves.
- All the qualities of music (its ability to move one emotionally, its sense of beauty, of completeness, its ability to calm) have as their source that series of sound waves.
- The language a musician uses to describe a piece of music is quite different from the language a physicist uses to describe sound waves.
- There is no hidden, secret music that exists alongside the sound waves – rather, the sound waves are the physical medium through which music is generated.
- **Therefore** it really should not be too difficult to see that the brain, along with the nervous system and all the physical activities (including speech) that it controls, is the physical medium through which a mind expresses itself.

There have been many subtle variations on the problem of how the body and mind are related, but most of them can be seen, in one way or another, to be a result of an attempt to express the interconnectedness and yet distinctness of physical and non-physical reality.

What is clear from recent neurophysics is that the brain is extremely complex, that it controls not just the autonomic nervous system, but also those elements that we describe as personality or mind.

It is equally clear that an essential feature of the mind is communication. It is difficult to see how one could describe a mind that did not communicate – and in communicating, by words, facial expressions, writing, the qualities of that mind are shared. It is no more sensible to try to analyse an isolated human brain in the hope of discovering the seeds of cultural history, than it is to take a Stradivarius apart in order to discover why a violin concerto can be so moving!

NEURONES AND COMPUTERS

To appreciate how the brain might be thought to create the mind, one can look at two different areas of computer science:

- **Artificial intelligence** (AI) uses computers to perform some of the functions of the human brain. It works on the basis of knowledge and response – the computer stores memories and is programmed to respond to present situations which correspond to them. It can, for example, recognize words, and can respond to them. The bigger the computer memory, the more 'lifelike' this form of artificial intelligence becomes.
- **Neural computing** goes about its task quite differently. It tries to produce a computer which actually works like a human brain – recognizing things, forming mental images, even dreaming and feeling emotions. A neural computer, although very simple by comparison, is like a brain in that it programmes itself and learns from its environment.

Some scientists claim that AI holds the key. The human brain, they argue, comprises about 100 million memories and a few thousand functions. All you need, in a sense, is raw computing power. On the other hand, this is never going to be that easy, because attempting to match the human brain – the most complex thing known in the universe – will take an enormous amount of computer power.

This view is countered by those who claim that neural computing holds the key to an understanding of the 'mind', since a neural computer can take on characteristics that are normally regarded as human. Human brains are not programmed, they just learn, and that is also the defining feature of neural computing.

Such discussions of artificial intelligence and neural networking take us well beyond the old mechanistic view of the universe, and therefore away from the kind of mind/body dualism that was introduced by Descartes. Intelligent activity is more likely to be seen now as a feature of complexity and of relationships. If something is complex enough, and if its operation is based on a constantly changing pattern of relationships between its memory components, then it appears to evolve in a personal and intelligent way; it takes on character.

KNOWING ME, KNOWING YOU

We now turn to some implications of the mind/body problem, particularly those that affect individuals in terms of their self-understanding, identity and knowledge of other people.

FREE WILL

Freedom of the will is a major feature in the mind/body debate. If, as a materialist or even a epiphenomenalist would claim, the mind is simply a by-product of brain activity, and if that brain activity, being part of a material world, is, in theory, totally predictable, then there is no such thing as free will. We appear to be free only because we do not understand the unique combination of causes which force us to make our particular decisions. We are pawns of fate – if all causes were known, we would have no freedom and no responsibility for what we (erroneously) call our 'mental' operations.

In effect, the issue here is exactly the same as **determinism** within the broader scope of the philosophy of science. We live in a world of cause and effect. If causality is universal (or if, as Kant, we believe that the mind automatically assumes that it is), then it provides a closed loop of explanation for everything that happens. Human beings and their choices, being part of the physical world, come within that loop.

Yet many people would want to argue that freedom and morality are an essential part of what it means to be a human individual. We are not robots, even sophisticated ones. Our role in the world is proactive, not reactive. We shape the world as much as we are shaped by it. From this perspective, it is difficult to see the mind as 'nothing more than' a by-product of brain activity.

KNOWLEDGE OF OTHER MINDS

In a strictly dualistic view of bodies and minds, you cannot have direct knowledge of the minds of others. You can know their words, their actions, their writings, their facial and other body signals, but you cannot get access to their minds. For a dualist, knowledge of other minds therefore comes by analogy. I know what it is like to be me. I know that, when I speak, I am expressing something that I am thinking. Therefore, I assume that, when another person speaks, his or her words are similarly the product of mental activity.

The meeting of two minds, as well as bodies?

From Ryle's point of view there is no problem. There is no 'ghost in the machine'; what we mean by 'mind' is the intelligent and communicative abilities of the other person. If I know his or her actions, words, etc., then I know his or her mind; the two things are one and the same.

Knowing oneself is rather different, in that we are immediately aware of our own thoughts, whereas the thoughts of others come to us via their words, gestures and appearance. This has led some people to argue that we can know only our own mind, and are therefore radically alone, surrounded by bodies in which we have to infer that there are other minds similar to our own.

Such a lonely view is termed **solipsism**, and this is the fate of those who think of the soul or mind as a crude, unknowable 'ghost', as caricatured by Ryle.

PERSONAL IDENTITY

There are many ways of identifying yourself:

- son or daughter of —
- a member of a particular school, university, business
- a citizen of a country, member of a race
- an earthling (if you happen to be travelling through space, this might become a very relevant way of describing yourself).

At various times, each of these will become more or less relevant for the purpose of self-identity. Relationships establish a sense of identity, and the closer the relationship, the more significant will be its influence on the sense of self. Aristotle held that friendships were essential for a sense of identity.

In practice, identity is not a matter of body or mind only, but of an integrated functioning entity comprising both body and mind. Of course, once the process of analysis starts, it is difficult to find a 'self' that is not at the same time something else – but that is exactly the reason why identity is not a matter of analysis.

- **Analysis** shows bits and pieces, none of which is 'you'.
- **Synthesis** shows the way in which body, mind and social function all come together in a unique combination – and that is 'you'.

Identity is therefore a matter of synthesis, not of analysis. *You are the sum total*, not the parts.

There is much that can be explored in terms of 'persons'. In recent philosophy this has been brought to attention by the work of P.F. Strawson (1919–2006), a British philosopher known particularly for his work on the nature of identity, and for his exposition and development of the philosophy of Immanuel Kant. In 'Persons', an article first published in 1958, and *Individuals* (1959) he argued that the concept of 'person' was prior to the popular analysis of it as an animated body, or an embodied mind. Rather, a person is such that both physical characteristics and states of consciousness can be ascribed to it. The concept of a 'person' has many practical and ethical implications:

- In what sense, and at what point, can an unborn child be called a person?
- An unborn child has a brain, but cannot communicate directly. Is such communication necessary for it to be called a full human being? (Consider also the case of the severely handicapped. Does lack of communication detract from their being termed 'people'?)
- Does a baby have to be independent before being classified as a person? If so, do we cease to be human once we are rendered totally dependent on others, for example on the operating table?
- What is the status of a person who goes into a coma?

COGNITIVE SCIENCE

Much of what we have been discussing in today's chapter is related to the traditional mind/body problem, which developed out of the radical dualism of Descartes and the issues raised by it. By the latter part of the twentieth century, however, these problems (without necessarily being resolved) were set in a new and broader context which is generally known as cognitive science.

Cognitive science is an umbrella term for a number of disciplines which impinge upon ideas of the self or mind:

- We have already considered the impact of computers on our understanding of mental process, and the development of AI and neural networking.
- Neuroscience is now able to map out the functions of the brain, identifying areas that are associated with particular mental or sensory processes.
- Pharmacology is able to control behaviour by the use of drugs, bringing a whole new chemical element into our understanding of behaviour.
- There is an increased awareness of the influence of food additives and environment in influencing mental activity; how we feel may well reflect what we eat and drink.
- Clinical psychology looks at the way an individual's mind functions, taking into account both its conscious and unconscious workings.

Clearly, there is no scope within this present book for examining all these disciplines. All we need to be aware of is the way in which science today is far more flexible in its approach to the mind than would have been the case a century or more ago.

A key term here is **functionalism**. This approach sees mental operations as the way in which intelligent life sorts out how to react to the stimuli it receives. Let us take a crude example. If I put my hand on something hot, my body receives the sensation of burning. My mind then becomes aware of the pain, remembers that, if the hand is not removed from the heat, damage is likely to be done, and therefore decides that I should withdraw my hand. Muscles contract, the hand is withdrawn, and the pain subsides. We may not be able to tell exactly which neurones, firing in the brain, were responsible for each step in that operation. What we do know, however, is the mental functions that were performed. Mind is what mind does.

Hence, a functionalist is able to produce what amounts to a map of the mind; a map that shows the different functions that the mind performs. What it cannot do, and argues that it is not necessary to do, is to wait to find out what each physical or electrical component does in the chain of events, before the significance of the mental function can be appreciated.

Intentionality

The idea of intentionality predates cognitive science, but is relevant to the broad range of issues that it considers. It originated in the work of the nineteenth-century psychologist Franz Brentano (1838–1917) and influenced the philosopher and psychologist William James (1842–1910). Intentionality, put simply, is the recognition that every perception and every experience is directed towards something. I do not just experience the shape of an apple before me, but I experience it as something to eat. In other words, mental functions shape and interpret what we experience – and we cannot have experience except as experience 'of' something.

Experience is about living in the world, relating to it, getting what we need from it, influencing it. It is not a separate and detached play of passing sense data. The mind takes an 'intentional stance' towards what it experiences.

SUMMARY

Today we have delved into one of the most enduring – and engaging – problems of philosophy – the nature and status of the mind. Should we consider the mind as something radically separate from the body, a hidden 'self' or even 'soul' that can exist even without or beyond the body? Or is it nothing more or less than a material part of the body, something, indeed, pretty much synonymous with the brain? Most philosophers, we have seen, adopt a position somewhere between these two notions, arguing that mind and body are different in kind, but nonetheless related. As we have seen, however, this opens up plenty more cans of worms.

The mind–body conundrum has a significance way beyond the sometimes arcane arguments of philosophers. If our minds are subject to our bodies – and not vice versa – then how can we have any responsibility for our actions? And if our minds float free of our bodies – unseen and undecipherable – how can we ever say that we know another person? Last but not least,

SUNDAY

MONDAY

TUESDAY

WEDNESDAY

THURSDAY

FRIDAY

SATURDAY

we have looked at how the philosophy of mind has powerful implications for ethics, the subject we will turn to on Friday.

Before that, though, let's examine an area that preoccupied the minds of medieval, Renaissance and Enlightenment philosophers, but which in more recent times has rather fallen from grace – the philosophy of religion.

FACT-CHECK (ANSWERS AT THE BACK)

1. What is the name given to the idea that the body and mind are distinct but related realities?
a) Materialism ❑
b) Realism ❑
c) Dualism ❑
d) Idealism ❑

2. What is solipsism?
a) A nasty disease ❑
b) The logical conclusion of idealism ❑
c) A kind of locked-in syndrome of the mind ❑
d) None of the above ❑

3. What objection did Ryle make to dualism? It is...
a) Simplistic ❑
b) A category mistake ❑
c) A linguistic muddle ❑
d) All of the above ❑

4. Which of the following describe(s) artificial intelligence (AI)?
a) It mimics the human brain ❑
b) It stores memories ❑
c) It performs the functions of a human brain ❑
d) It responds to situations it has been programmed to respond to ❑

5. Which of the following describe(s) neural intelligence?
a) It mimics the human mind ❑
b) It feels emotions ❑
c) It performs functions in the same way as a human brain ❑
d) It programmes itself ❑

6. A purely materialist point of view makes free will...
a) Possible ❑
b) Unlikely ❑
c) Impossible ❑
d) Probable ❑

7. Following a strictly dualist point of view, knowing others' minds is possible only by...
a) Imagination ❑
b) Brain surgery ❑
c) Analogy ❑
d) It's impossible! ❑

8. Which philosopher developed the concept of the 'person' so influential in contemporary ethics?
a) Kant ❑
b) Ryle ❑
c) Strawson ❑
d) Descartes ❑

9. Which of the following disciplines are included under the term 'cognitive science'?
a) Neurology ❑
b) Psychology ❑
c) Neuroscience ❑
d) Computer science ❑

10. How might we best define intentionality?
a) Another term for free will ❑
b) Experience is always about or of something ❑
c) Our actions are always intentional ❑
d) None of the above ❑

THURSDAY

The
philosophy
of religion

The philosophy of religion offers a rational examination of religious language, religious experience and the belief claims made by religious people. It is centrally concerned with the question of what people mean by 'God' and whether any such god can be said to exist.

It also explores questions about whether religious claims can withstand scientific scrutiny, whether miracles can happen, whether belief in God is compatible with the fact of suffering and evil, and whether psychological and sociological explanations of religion render religious belief redundant.

In today's chapter we shall examine just one of the arguments for the existence of God – the argument from design – noting its limitations and how it relates to a scientific view of the world. We shall then move on to examine the greatest challenge to any such belief, namely that of finding a rational way of reconciling a loving and omnipotent creator with the experience of suffering.

KEY QUESTIONS

In Western thought, the philosophy of religion is concerned with:

- **religious language:** what it means, what it does and whether it can be shown to be true or false
- **metaphysical claims** (e.g. that God exists): the nature of the arguments by which such claims are defended, and the basis upon which those claims can be shown to be true or false.

In addition to these basic areas of study, there are many questions concerning religious beliefs and practices which philosophy can examine:

- What is faith? How does it relate to reason? Is it ever reasonable to be a religious 'fundamentalist'?
- What is 'religious experience' and what sort of knowledge can it yield?
- Is the universe such as to suggest that it has an intelligent creator and designer?
- Are miracles possible? If so, could we ever have sufficient evidence to prove that?
- Is belief in a loving God compatible with the existence of suffering and evil in the world?
- Can psychology explain the phenomenon of religion?
- Is life after death possible? If so, what difference does it make to our view of life?

FAITH, REASON AND BELIEF

Is religious belief based on reason? If it were, it would be open to change, if the logic of an argument went against it. However, experience tells us that most religious people hold beliefs that, while they may be open to reasonable scrutiny, depend on a prior commitment or wish to believe, and therefore belief may persist in the face of reasonable criticism.

Within Christianity, there is a tradition – associated particularly with the Protestant Reformation and Calvin – that human nature is fallen and sinful, and that human reason is equally limited and unable to yield knowledge of God. Belief in

God is therefore a matter of faith, and any logical arguments to back that belief are secondary.

Reason, emotion or what?

Debates between atheists and believers are often frustrating. The one expects that reason and evidence will settle the matter; the other has deep emotional and intuitive 'reasons' for believing. But the key question is: Can you believe 'in' something, if you do not also have reasons to believe 'that' it exists? Is spiritual intuition enough?

The quest for certainty is sometimes termed **foundationalism** – the attempt to find statements that are so obviously true that they cannot be challenged. We have already seen that Descartes came to his incontrovertible statement 'I think, therefore I am.' Some modern philosophers of religion, notably Alvin Plantinga, argue for a 'Reformed Epistemology'. That is, a theory of knowledge that, like the theologians of the Reformation, is based on basic beliefs that are self-evident to the person who holds them, even if they are not open to reasoned argument. An example of this would be the belief that the universe is designed by God, based on a sense of wonder and beauty. We shall look at the 'design argument' a little later; what is different here is that Plantinga thinks that such belief is not a logical conclusion to an argument, but is held *prior* to engaging with that argument.

A related idea is **fundamentalism**. Originally used as a term for those who wished to set aside the superficialities of religion and return to its fundamental principles, it is now more commonly used for those who take beliefs, as they are found in the Bible or the Qur'an for example, in a very literal and straightforward sense and apply them without allowing them to be challenged by reason. A basic problem with this is that the scriptures were written using particular language and in a particular context, and if statements are taken literally and out of context, the original intention of the writers may be lost.

Of course, the fundamentalist would not accept this, believing that the words of scripture are given directly by God and are therefore not open to any form of literary or contextual analysis.

That something more than logic is needed if we are to understand the nature of religious statements was highlighted by the Danish philosopher Søren Kierkegaard (1813–55). He argued that a 'leap of faith' was necessary, and that it was not so much the content of a belief that made it religious, but the way in which it is believed – with subjectivity and inwardness.

DOES GOD EXIST?

Since we are concerned with Western philosophy, the relevant concepts have come from the Western theistic religions – Judaism, Christianity and Islam. For these, God may be said to be a supreme being, infinite, spiritual and personal, creator of the world. He is generally described as all-powerful (having created the world out of nothing, he can do anything he wishes) and all-loving (in a personal caring relationship with individual believers). Although pictured in human form, he is believed to be beyond literal description (and is thus not strictly male, although 'he' is generally depicted as such).

Some terms

- Belief in the existence of such a god is **theism**.
- The conviction that no such being exists is **atheism**.
- The view that there is no conclusive evidence to decide whether God exists or not is **agnosticism**.
- An identification of God with the physical universe is **pantheism**.
- The belief that God is within everything and everything within God (but God and the physical universe are not simply identified) is **panentheism**. (Although this term is used by some theologians, most interpretations of theism include the idea of everything being 'within' God; indeed, if he is infinite, there is nothing which is external to him.)
- The idea of an external designer God who created the world, but is not immanent within it, is **deism**.

There is a problem with taking the idea of the existence of God too literally. Thomas Aquinas described God as being *supra ordinem omnium entium* – beyond the order of all beings. In other words, God is not a being who might or might not exist somewhere; indeed, he is not a being at all. So we should not be tempted (as are some evangelical atheists) to assume a crude idea of God and then show that there is no evidence for his existence. On those terms, Aquinas and most serious religious thinkers down through the centuries would certainly have qualified as atheists. The meaning of God is far more subtle than that.

THE ARGUMENT FROM DESIGN

Although Aquinas has a form of this argument, the clearest example of it is that of William Paley (1743–1805). He argued that, if he were to find a watch lying on the ground, he would assume that it was the product of a designer, for, unlike a stone, he would see at once that it was made up of many different parts worked together in order to produce movement, and that, if any one part were ordered differently, the whole thing would not work. In the same way, he argued that the world is like a machine, each part of it designed so that it takes its place within the whole. If the world is so designed, it must have a designer whose purpose is expressed through it.

This argument, reflecting the sense of wonder at nature, was most seriously challenged by the theory of evolution. Darwin's 'natural selection' provided an alternative explanation for design, and one that did not require the aid of any external designer. At once, it became possible to see the world not as a machine, but as a process of struggle and death in which those best adapted to their environment were able to breed and pass their genes on to the next generation, thus influencing the very gradual development of the species. Adaptation in order to survive became the key to the development of the most elaborate forms, which previously would have been described as an almost miraculous work of a designer God.

Actually, the challenge of natural selection was anticipated in the work of Hume, who set out a criticism of the design argument some 23 years before Paley published his version of it. He argued that, in a finite world and given infinite time, any combination of things can occur. Those combinations that work together harmoniously can continue and thrive, those that do not will fail. Therefore, when we come to observe the world as it is now, we are observing only those that do work, for those that don't are no longer there to be observed. The implication of this is that we observe a world populated by survivors, but that does not mean that it is so ordered by an external designer; it is merely the result of a long period of time and endless failures.

- **If** you prove that God 'exists' in a way that would satisfy a logical positivist (i.e. testable by empirical evidence)
- **Then** 'God' becomes part of the world
- **So** he is no longer 'God'.

So you might call yourself a theist, but a religious person would be more likely to say that your belief was no more than idolatry. It is also worth remembering that idolatry is not simply a matter of worshipping a physical image. A person may claim to believe in 'God' when in fact he or she actually believes in a particular idea of God, not the source of reality itself. That is a very common form of idolatry. Indeed, many religious wars come about when conflicting ideas are elevated to divine status, and people feel the need to defend them as though they were defending 'God' himself, which – in the broader perspective – does seem a particularly silly thing to try to do!

This is an important thing to keep in mind, because it might be possible to see the arguments for the existence of God as either succeeding or failing to give definitive proof of the objective existence of an entity to which the name 'God' can be given. This is simplistic, and is only part of the issue. More important is to ask what part such arguments play in the religious perception of the believer.

Generally speaking, the arguments show the sort of place the idea of God has in terms of the perception of the world – to say that he is uncaused cause, or the designer of the world, is to locate God in the realm of overall meaning and purpose. Such convictions express a view that is unlikely to be changed (but could be strengthened) by the traditional arguments.

The problem is that, once God is given a role in the origin and design of the universe, any alternative scientific theories that explain the same things without requiring any supernatural agency, may be seen as threats to religious belief. Hence, at a superficial level, religion would seem to have a vested interest in the failure of science to give a complete explanation of the universe. On the other hand, it is clear that many scientists – in the past and also today – do hold religious beliefs and certainly do not see their scientific work as in any sense incompatible with them.

So we need to ask: Are the religious and scientific approaches to these topics compatible?

In *The Blind Watchmaker* (1986), Richard Dawkins makes the point that the argument for the world being made by an intelligent designer is based on the assumption that complexity cannot arise spontaneously. How then can an organized and complex designer exist without further explanation and cause? Surely, it is just as easy to accept that the complex organization of the world can appear spontaneously as it is to accept that a complex designer can appear spontaneously. But his central theme is that the process of natural selection gives us a mechanism which explains how complexity can arise from original simplicity. Once you accept that, there is no need to look for an external cause for design. Dawkins' point is not that belief in a creator can be disproved; rather, he shows that the idea is superfluous. This has been the principal threat to religious belief in a designer-god, ever since Charles Darwin put forward the theory of natural selection – for that theory put forward the first genuinely independent explanation of the appearance of design.

But this argument does not deny the sense of wonder at the beauty and complexity of the world. Indeed, Dawkins himself (in *Unweaving the Rainbow*) expresses amazement at what can arise from what is basically a mathematical sequence. Light and colour are no less impressive for being susceptible to scientific analysis.

The fundamental question therefore is: Can the world (in theory, if not in practice) provide us with an explanation of itself? If it can, this aspect of religion appears superfluous. If it cannot, is that because ...

- Our minds are incapable of understanding any overall cause for that within which we are immersed?

or

- The explanation can only come through religious intuition (or the direct revelation of God) rather than through human reason and science?

THE PROBLEM OF EVIL

In its simplest form, the problem can be stated like this:

- **If** God created the world
- **And** if God is all-powerful and all-loving
- **Then** why is there evil and suffering in the world?

Conclusion:

- **Either** God is not all-powerful
- **Or** God is not all-loving
- **Or** suffering is either unreal, necessary or a means to a greater good
- **Or** the whole idea of an all-loving and all-powerful creator God was a mistake in the first place.

An important book setting out suggested answers to this problem is *Evil and the God of Love* (1966) by John Hick (1922–2012), a philosopher and theologian notable for his contribution to the problem of evil and also to the issue of religious pluralism. In that book he gives two main lines of approach, the Augustinian and the Irenaean:

1 The Augustinian approach is named after St Augustine (354–430), and reflects his background in Neoplatonism. In Plato's thought, particular things are imperfect copies of their 'Forms'. Imperfection is a feature of the world as we experience it. The Augustinian approach to evil and suffering is to say that evil is not a separate force opposing the good, but is a lack of goodness, a deprivation. The world as we experience it is full of imperfect copies, and suffering and evil are bound up with that imperfection.

How can we reconcile human suffering and an omnipotent and good god?

2 The Irenaean approach is named after Bishop Irenaeus of Lyons (c.130–c.202). It presents the idea that human life is imperfect, but having been made in the image of God, human beings are intended to grow and develop, aspiring to be what God intended them to be. Through free will and all the sufferings of life, people have an opportunity to grow and learn.

Hick's own approach to the problem of evil is one that treats evil as something to be tackled and overcome, but with the hope that, ultimately, it will be seen as part of an overall divine plan.

The crucial difference between the religious and non-religious evaluation of life, is that – in general – the non-religious approach is that life is of value in itself, not as a preparation for anything beyond this world. The challenge of atheism is the challenge of acceptance of a limited life with an unequally distributed mixture of pleasure and pain.

To say 'yes' to this life, just as it is, and to be prepared to live this life over and over again, just as it is, is the hallmark of someone radically free from the consolations of religion. Indeed, Nietzsche made such 'yes-saying' a key feature of his Übermensch (superman), the higher form to which humankind is challenged to evolve.

SUMMARY

Today we have taken the plunge into the philosophy of religion, which examines rational arguments about religious belief and metaphysical questions about the nature and existence of God. One of the key thinkers here is Thomas Aquinas, who attempted to show that Christian belief was compatible with the philosophy of Aristotle and set out five famous proofs for the existence of God (one of which we have covered here, though in a form put forward by William Paley). A great deal of attention has also been paid to the 'problem of evil' – that is, how to reconcile the idea of an omnipotent and loving god with a world in which there is suffering and evil.

As we have seen in earlier chapters, such metaphysical questions have been criticized in some modern Western philosophy as being unsusceptible to rational analysis. Nietzsche famously declared that 'God is dead', while Wittgenstein claimed, at the end of Tractatus, that 'whereof one cannot speak, thereof one must be silent' – putting limits on any attempt to describe anything beyond the world of our sense experience.

SUNDAY

MONDAY

TUESDAY

WEDNESDAY

THURSDAY

FRIDAY

SATURDAY

Nevertheless, there is still lively debate among philosophers about religious questions. Although few would defend the literal interpretation of religious beliefs, most recognize that religious issues are interesting both intellectually and as a way of exploring how people have tried to find meaning and significance in life.

FACT-CHECK (ANSWERS AT THE BACK)

1. In Christian thought, reason is often portrayed as...
a) Equal to faith ❏
b) Limited ❏
c) Secondary to faith ❏
d) Unlimited ❏

2. What is foundationalism?
a) Going back to basics ❏
b) An attempt to find unchallengeable statements ❏
c) The assertion of fundamental beliefs from which all other knowledge derives ❏
d) None of the above ❏

3. Kierkegaard argued that religion required...
a) A jump of reason ❏
b) Fear and trembling ❏
c) The renunciation of reason ❏
d) A leap of faith ❏

4. What is pantheism? The belief that...
a) God is everywhere ❏
b) God and the universe are the same thing ❏
c) God created everything ❏
d) All of the above ❏

5. What is deism? The belief that...
a) God created everything ❏
b) God is everywhere ❏
c) God is not involved directly in the world ❏
d) All of the above ❏

6. Darwin's theory of natural selection challenged the design argument for the existence of God because:
a) It showed that design was incompatible with God ❏
b) It provided a natural explanation for the appearance of design ❏
c) It showed that the world was too complex to have been designed ❏
d) All of the above ❏

7. How might we best sum up the 'problem of evil'?
a) An attempt to define evil ❏
b) An attempt to explain the existence of sin ❏
c) An attempt to reconcile the idea of a good, all-powerful god with the sufferings of humanity ❏
d) None of the above ❏

8. How did St Augustine explain the existence of evil?
a) As the absence of good ❏
b) As a force in opposition to the good ❏
c) As a result of human erring ❏
d) None of the above ❏

9. How did Irenaeus explain the existence of evil?
a) Human beings are irredeemably 'fallen' ❑
b) An imperfect world challenges human beings to grow and develop ❑
c) As a test for human beings ❑
d) Humans are made in the image of God, who encompasses both good and evil ❑

10. What is the approach of John Hick to this same problem?
a) It is similar to St Augustine's ❑
b) Evil is something to be tackled and overcome ❑
c) 'Evil' does not exist ❑
d) None of the above ❑

SUNDAY

MONDAY

TUESDAY

WEDNESDAY

THURSDAY

FRIDAY

SATURDAY

FRIDAY

Ethics

Normative ethics, the study of issues of right and wrong, recognizes that what we 'ought' to do goes beyond (and cannot be justified by) statements about the facts of human behaviour. It also presupposes freedom of choice; if we are not free, we cannot be blamed.

In today's chapter we look at three broad types of moral theory – natural law, which considers a rational interpretation of nature and purpose; utilitarianism, which judges moral decisions according to their expected results, and Kantian ethics, which presents abstract, universal moral principles.

We shall also consider moral relativity, both in terms of seeing every moral decision against its background, and also the way in which morality is shaped by the society within which it develops.

Finally, today, we look briefly at virtue ethics, which explores the way in which the virtues enable human flourishing. The important thing, in gaining an appreciation of these theories and perspectives, is to be able to apply them to practical moral situations.

Once you start to talk about morality, or about the purpose of things, you introduce matters of value as well as those of fact. An important question for philosophy is whether it is possible to derive values from facts, or whether facts must always remain 'neutral'. In other words:

- Facts say what 'is'.
- Values say what 'ought' to be.

This leads to the question:

- Can we ever derive an 'ought' from an 'is'?

If the answer to this question is 'no', then how are we to decide issues of morality? If no facts can be used to establish morality, can there be absolute moral rules, or are all moral decisions relative, dependent upon particular circumstances, feelings or desires?

FREEDOM AND DETERMINISM

One of the fundamental issues of philosophy is freedom and determinism. It is also related to reductionism – the reduction of complex entities (like human beings) to the simpler parts of which they are composed. If we are nothing more than the individual cells that comprise our bodies, and if those cells are determined by physical forces and are predictable, then there seems no room for the whole human being to exercise freedom.

For now, dealing with ethics, one distinction is clear:

- If we are free to make a choice, then we can be responsible for what we do. Praise or blame are appropriate. We can act on the basis of values that we hold.
- If we are totally conditioned, we have no choice in what we do, and it makes no sense to speak of moral action springing from choices and values, or action being worthy of praise or blame.

In considering the moral implications of actions, we have to assess the degree of freedom available to the agent.

We are all conditioned by many factors – there is no doubt of that. The difference between that and determinism is that determinism leaves no scope for human freedom and choice (we are automata), whereas those who argue against determinism claim that there remains a measure of freedom that is exercised within the prevailing conditions.

KINDS OF ETHICAL LANGUAGE

DESCRIPTIVE ETHICS

This is the most straightforward form of ethical language. It is simply a description of what happens: what moral choices are made and in which particular circumstances. Rather than making a statement about the rights or wrongs of abortion, for example, descriptive ethics simply gives facts and figures about how many abortions take place, how they are carried out, and what legal restraints are placed on that practice. *Descriptive ethics is about 'is' rather than 'ought'.*

NORMATIVE ETHICS

Normative ethics deals with the norms of action, in terms of whether an action is considered good or bad, right or wrong. It expresses values and makes a moral judgement based on them. It may relate to facts, but it is not wholly defined by facts. It may be justified in a number of ways that we shall examine shortly. *Normative ethics is about 'ought'; it makes judgements.*

META-ETHICS

When philosophy examines the claims made in normative ethics, a number of questions are raised:

● What does it mean to say that something is right or wrong?
● Can moral statements be said to be either true or false?
● Do they express more than the preferences of the person who makes them?
● What is the meaning of the terms used in ethical discourse?

These questions are not themselves moral statements; they do not say that any particular thing is right or wrong. Meta-ethics is a branch of philosophy which does to normative ethical statement what philosophy does to language in general. It examines ethical language to find out what it means and how it is used.

THREE BASES FOR ETHICS

If moral language is simply expressing an emotion or a preference, then it does not seem to need further justification; it implies no more than the feelings of the moment. If we want to argue for a moral position, however, we need to find a rational basis for ethics. Within the history of Western philosophy there have been three principal bases offered: **natural law, utilitarianism** and the **categorical imperative**. We shall examine each of these in turn.

I NATURAL LAW

In Book 1 of *Nicomachean Ethics*, Aristotle says:

> *Every art and every enquiry, and similarly every action and pursuit, is thought to aim at some good; and for this reason the good has rightly been declared to be that at which all things aim.*
>
> p.1094a

Aristotle develops this into the idea of the supreme good for human beings: happiness (*eudaimonia*). If you agree with Aristotle that everything has a final cause or purpose, a 'good' for which it exists, or if you accept with Plato that the 'Forms' (especially the 'Form of the Good') have a permanent reality, independent of our own minds and perceptions, then it should be possible to specify which things are 'good' and which 'bad', which actions are 'right' and which 'wrong' in an independent and objective way.

Natural law is the approach to ethics which claims that something is right if it fulfils its true purpose in life, wrong if it goes against it.

Natural law is not the same as a consideration of what appears as a natural response to a situation – natural in the sense that it reflects the nature that humankind shares with the rest of the animal kingdom. Rather, it is *nature as seen through the eyes of reason*; indeed, for most of those who would use a natural law argument, it is also coloured by religious views, with the world seen as the purposeful creation by God.

2 UTILITARIANISM

Utilitarianism is a moral theory associated particularly with Jeremy Bentham (1748–1832), a philosopher, lawyer and social reformer, involved particularly with the practical issues of prison reform, education and the integrity of public institutions, and further developed by John Stuart Mill (1806–73), a campaigner for individual liberty and for the rights of women. Its roots, however, are found earlier in the basic idea of hedonism.

Hedonism is the term used for a philosophy which makes the achievement of happiness the prime goal in life. Epicurus taught in Athens at the end of the fourth century BCE. He took an atomistic view of the world (everything is composed of indivisible atoms), regarded the gods as having little influence on life, and generally considered the main purpose of life to be the gaining of pleasure, in the broad sense of wellbeing. Pain, he held, was of shorter duration than pleasure, and death was nothing but the dissolution of the atoms of which we are made, with no afterlife to fear. He therefore considered that the wise should lead a life free from anxiety, and if morality had any purpose it was to maximize the amount of wellbeing that life can offer.

This was to become the basis of utilitarian theories of ethics: that the right thing to do on any occasion is that which aims to give maximum happiness to all concerned. This may be expressed in the phrase 'the greatest good for the greatest number', and Bentham made the point that everyone should count equally in such an assessment – a radical point of view for him to take at that time. Utilitarianism is therefore a theory *based on the expected results of an action, rather than any inherent sense of right or wrong.*

Utilitarians see ethics as the maximization of wellbeing.

This is very much a common-sense view of ethics; to do what is right is often associated with doing what will benefit the majority. From a philosophical point of view, however, there are certain problems associated with it:

- You can never be certain what the total effects of an action are going to be. To take a crude example: you may save the life of a drowning child, who then grows up to be a mass murderer. In practice, there always has to be a cut-off point beyond which it is not practicable to calculate consequences. Added to this is the fact that we see the result of actions only with hindsight; at the time, we might have expected something quite different. Thus, although utilitarianism seems to offer a straightforward way of assessing moral issues, its assessment must always remain provisional.
- The definition of what constitutes happiness may not be objective. Other people may not want what you deem to be their happiness or in their best interests. The utilitarian argument appears to make a factual consideration of results the basis of moral choice, but in practice, in selecting the

degree or type of happiness to be considered, a person is already making value (and perhaps moral) judgements.

● How do you judge between pain caused to a single individual and the resulting happiness of many others? Would global benefit actually justify the inflicting of pain on a single innocent person?

Without doubt, utilitarianism is the most popular ethical theory today – and one that, to many people, is taken as common sense. It can be used to present radical moral challenges, as for example in the many books by Peter Singer (b. 1946), who argues that you should give equal consideration to others as to yourself. Thus, if you are able to prevent something bad from happening to another person, without thereby sacrificing anything morally significant to yourself, you should always do so. This has huge implications for tackling the issue of world poverty. He asks how one can morally justify retaining wealth in a situation where one is aware of the benefits it can offer others. The problem, of course, is that it seems 'natural' to care for yourself and your family and friends more than those who live at a distance and are not known personally; but it is difficult to give a rational justification for the resulting disparity in wealth and chances in life.

Both utilitarianism and natural law appear to give rational and objective bases for deciding between right and wrong. Both of them, however, have presuppositions which are not accounted for by the theory itself. One depends on the idea of a rational final cause, the other on the acceptance of wellbeing of all as the highest good.

THE CATEGORICAL IMPERATIVE

We have already looked at the work of the eighteenth-century German philosopher Kant in connection with the radical distinction he made between things as we perceive them and things as they are in themselves, and the categories of space, time and causality by which we interpret our experience. But Kant also made an important contribution in the field of ethics. He sought to formulate a general and universally applicable principle by which pure practical reason could distinguish right from wrong.

Kant started with the fact that people have a sense of moral obligation – what he calls the **categorical imperative**. In other words, we all know that there are things we 'should' do, irrespective of the consequences. He contrasted this with a 'hypothetical' imperative, which says what you need to do in order to achieve some chosen result. Thus:

- You should work hard (categorical imperative).
- You should work hard if you want to succeed in this business (hypothetical imperative).

Kant's aim was to express this experience of the categorical imperative in the form of universal principles of morality. These principles are generally referred to as the three forms of Kant's categorical imperative. He expressed them using various forms of words, but they amount to this:

1 Act only on that maxim (or principle) which you can – at the same time – will that it should become a universal law.
2 Act in such a way as to treat people as ends and never as means.
3 Act as though you were legislating for a kingdom of ends.

The first of these expresses the idea that, whatever one wishes to do, one should be prepared for everyone else to act upon that same principle. If you are not prepared for the maxim of your action to become a universal rule, then you should not do it in your individual circumstances.

The second form of the categorical imperative follows from the first. If you want to express your own moral autonomy, you should treat all others on the basis that they would want the same. So you should not treat them as 'means' to your own end, but as 'ends' in themselves. And the third form suggests that you should make your moral judgements as though you had responsibility for legislating in a kingdom in which everyone was an 'end', respected as an autonomous moral being.

ABSOLUTE OR RELATIVE MORALITY?

If moral rules are absolute, then a particular action may be considered wrong no matter what the circumstances. So, for

Never treat people as means...

example, theft may be considered to be wrong. But what is theft? In one sense, the definition is straightforward: theft is the action of taking what belongs to another without that person's consent. The problem is that 'theft' is a term that may be used to interpret individual situations. Can we always be sure that it is the right term? If not, then is it right to treat an action as morally equal to 'theft', if that is not the way one or more of the people concerned see the matter.

One example of this dilemma might be 'mercy killing', where someone who is seriously ill and facing the prospect of a painful or lingering death is helped to die by a relative or close friend. If you take a view that there are moral absolutes, you may say: 'Murder is always wrong.' The next question then becomes: 'Is mercy killing the same thing as murder?' In other words, you start with absolute moral principles and then assess each particular situation in terms of which of these moral principles are involved (a process that is generally termed **casuistry**).

If you do not think that there are moral absolutes, you are more likely to start with particular situations and assess the intentions and consequences involved. In making such an assessment, you bring to bear your general views about life and of the implications that various actions have on society as a whole.

There is a broader sense in which we need to be aware of relativity in ethics. Each society has its own particular way of life, along with the values and principles that are expressed in it. What might be considered right in one society may be thought wrong in another. A set of moral rules may be drawn up that are valid for a particular society, but cannot be applied universally.

But the real problem for many ethical thinkers today is with a full-blown relativism which simply refuses to accept any general moral norms. In other words, it becomes increasingly difficult to make any moral judgements that may not be challenged on the basis of the gender, race, religion or social position of the person making that judgement. Sensitivity to social norms or particular circumstances has always been a key feature of ethics – and even the much maligned process of 'casuistry' attempted to apply moral principles to particular situations rather than impose them. But at some point, if moral discussions are to be effective, there needs to be a shared set of values, and that implies that there must be a limit to relativism.

VIRTUE ETHICS

Rather than looking at actions, and asking if they are right or wrong, one could start by asking the basic question 'What does it mean to be a "good" person?', and develop this to explore the qualities and virtues that make up the 'good' life. This approach had been taken first by Aristotle, who linked the displaying of certain qualities with the final end or purpose of life.

As it developed in the 1950s, this approach appealed to feminist thinkers, who considered the traditional ethical arguments to have been influenced by particularly male ways of approaching life, based on rights and duties, whereas they sought a more 'feminine' approach and a recognition of the value of relationships and intimacy.

Virtue ethics was also seen as 'naturalistic', in that it moved away from the idea of simply obeying rules, to an appreciation of how one might express one's own fundamental nature, and thus fulfil one's potential as a human being.

Virtue ethics raises some basic questions:

- Do we have a fixed *essence*? Are there particular masculine or feminine qualities that give rise to virtues appropriate to each sex? Or is our nature the product of our surroundings and upbringing?
- If our nature has been shaped by factors over which we have no control (e.g. the culture into which we have been born, traumatic experiences in childhood), *are we responsible for our actions*?
- How should we relate the expression of an individual's virtues to the actual needs of society?
- How are you able to decide between different ways of expressing the same virtue? For example, a sense of love and compassion might lead one person to help someone who is seriously ill to die, yet another might find that love and compassion lead them to struggle to keep that same person alive. In some way, you need to fall back on other ethical theories if you want to assess the actions that spring from particular virtues.

SUMMARY

Ethics, we have seen today, is a huge subject – both in terms of the range of ethical theories and the way in which these may be applied to moral and social issues. It has provided the impetus for much work in philosophy as a whole, and is the single largest area of study within departments of philosophy (judging by the number of papers published). It is particularly valuable as an area of philosophical study, since the benefits of clear thinking, analysis and the clarification of concepts and presuppositions can be seen to have immediate relevance to practical areas of life.

Faced with the dilemma of whether or not to turn off the life-support machine of someone in a deep coma and unable to recover, one starts to ask not just about the ethical status of euthanasia, but also what it means to be a human being, what constitutes human life, and therefore whether the person whose body is being maintained by a machine can be said to be living in any meaningful way.

Tomorrow we turn to our final subject for this week – political philosophy.

SUNDAY

MONDAY

TUESDAY

WEDNESDAY

THURSDAY

FRIDAY

SATURDAY

FACT-CHECK (ANSWERS AT THE BACK)

1. Ethics deals with...
a) Facts ❏
b) Values ❏
c) Laws ❏
d) Rules ❏

2. To be an ethical agent, one must have...
a) Faith ❏
b) Money ❏
c) Free will ❏
d) Values ❏

3. Normative ethics...
a) Makes moral judgements ❏
b) Describes facts ❏
c) Defines what is normal ❏
d) Considers values ❏

4. Meta-ethics...
a) Interrogates the assumptions of normative ethics ❏
b) Emphasizes the role of religion in ethics ❏
c) Examines the language of ethics ❏
d) None of the above ❏

5. Utilitarianism is most closely associated with which philosopher?
a) Aristotle ❏
b) Kant ❏
c) Leibniz ❏
d) Bentham ❏

6. Utilitarianism makes ethical judgements based on...
a) Means ❏
b) Rules ❏
c) Duties ❏
d) Results ❏

7. Which of the following are problems for utilitarianism?
a) What constitutes a 'good' result is subjective ❏
b) It is impossible to predict all the results of an action ❏
c) It places too much emphasis on personal happiness ❏
d) All of the above ❏

8. Which philosopher developed the idea of the 'categorical' imperative?
a) Bentham ❏
b) Nietzche ❏
c) Hegel ❏
d) Kant ❏

9. In Kantian ethics, there is a duty to treat people as...
a) Ends ❏
b) Autonomous ethical beings ❏
c) Means ❏
d) As you would like to be treated yourself ❏

10. Virtue ethics emphasizes the importance of...
a) Results ❏
b) Character ❏
c) Abstract virtues ❏
d) Duties ❏

SATURDAY

Political philosophy

From this major branch of philosophy, today's chapter will explore two key theories: the first is the social contract, which formed the historical basis of modern democracy; the second is the Marxist view of the material basis of society and the agency of social change. Both have been hugely influential in shaping modern political thought.

Equally important is the concept of justice, which is fundamental to social ethics. We shall look briefly at one ancient approach (that of Plato) and two modern views (those of Rawls and Nozick). We shall also consider the balancing of freedom and the law, including Mill's view that one should be given maximum freedom provided harm is not done to others, and consider how human rights relate to the needs of society.

Finally, we shall look at the feminist perspective on the way in which a male-dominated society has attempted to define what it is to be a woman.

THE SOCIAL CONTRACT

Self-preservation is a fundamental human need. Born in 1588, Thomas Hobbes knew first hand the traumas of civil war in England and used such a lawless and dangerous state as the starting point for his political theory. In Chapter 13 of *Leviathan*, published in 1651, he considers what life is like when a person can rely only on his own strength for protection:

> *In such condition, there is no place for industry, because the fruit thereof is uncertain; and consequently no culture of the earth; no navigation, nor use of the commodities that may be imported by sea; no commodious building, no instruments of moving or removing such things as require much force; no knowledge of the face of the earth; no account of time; no arts; no letters; no society; and, which is worst of all, continual fear and danger of violent death; and the life of man solitary, poor, nasty, brutish, and short.*

Hobbes considered that the need for self-preservation was so basic to human life that (using a 'natural law' form of argument) reason could show that the basis for political science was the preservation of life. He also showed, in the passage just quoted, that society depends upon personal security, and that without it civilization is impossible.

In this situation, Hobbes argued that people would band together for their mutual protection, and would set up a ruler who would maintain order. The value of the state is seen in its ability to protect and benefit the individuals of which it is comprised. His political theory, the start of what is called the 'social contract' tradition, springs from this need for self-preservation. Hobbes believed, however, that the ruler so appointed should be given absolute power, and that only by doing so could the security of the state be maintained.

Hobbes's absolute ruler

John Locke (1632–1704) argued from a similar starting point.
He saw the laws imposed by a ruler on individuals as based
on the need for the preservation of life and private property
within the state, and defence from foreign threats. But he
went beyond Hobbes, arguing that the people who entered
into their social contract should have the right, if the rulers
did not benefit them, to replace them with others. In other
words, he argued for a representative democracy, with rulers
accountable to those who have put them in power. Thus we
have a constitutional government, where rulers have power,
but only to the extent that they are given it by the people, and
within principles that are set out within a constitution.

Such political systems are based on a social contract; on
the agreement between people that they shall act together for
their mutual benefit. The problem arises over exactly what is
to the benefit of society, and who is to decide it. To what extent
can an individual, on the basis of a social contract, act on
behalf of all? Do all have to agree before some action is taken?

On what basis is there to be arbitration between conflicting interests. Locke is clear that decisions must reflect the wishes of a majority, and any minority must accept that judgement:

> *Every man, by consenting with others to make one body politic under one government, puts himself under an obligation to every one of that society to submit to the determination of the majority, and to be concluded by it; or else this original compact, whereby he with others incorporates into one society, would signify nothing, and be no compact if he be left free and under no other ties than he was in before in the state of Nature.*

The Second Treatise of Government, Chapter 13, section 97

Thus a government can act as long as it has the consent of a majority. But what if a government seeks to act in a way which the rulers consider to be in the interests of the people, even if that is not what people as individuals actually want?

MARX AND MATERIALISM

Karl Marx (1818–83) has been an enormously influential thinker. Indeed, one cannot start to describe the history of the twentieth century without reference to Marxism and the communist regimes that sprang from it. Born in Germany, he moved to Paris when the newspaper he was editing was forced to close. Expelled from both Paris and then Brussels, he finally settled in London. His most important book, *Das Kapital* (1867), predicts that capitalism has within it the seeds of its own destruction and will give way to socialism.

Marx argued that religion, morality, political ideas and social structures were fundamentally rooted in economics, particularly the production and distribution of goods. People have basic needs which must be fulfilled in order for them to live, and society becomes more and more sophisticated in order to produce the goods and services to meet those needs. He therefore interpreted history in economic terms, as shaped by the struggle between different social classes. The bourgeoisie confronts the proletariat; employers facing employees as once landowners faced their peasants. Individual actions are judged by the way in which they contribute to the class struggle, and the actions of a class as a whole is seen in a broader context of the movement of society.

In terms of the history of philosophy, Marx was influenced by Georg Wilhelm Friedrich Hegel (1770–1831), who saw the lives of individuals as bound up with the tide of history, which itself was unfolding by a rational process. Like Hegel, Marx saw reality as working itself out through a process of change. Hegel had introduced the idea of a 'dialectic': first you have a thesis, then in response to this you have the opposite (an antithesis), and bringing these two together you get a synthesis. But, for Hegel, this process was non-material, leading to a harmonious awareness of the *Geist*, or spirit of the age, in which everyone freely accepts the interest of the whole of society.

For Marx, by contrast, the process of dialectic is material. It is the economic conditions under which the classes live and work that produce the urge to change, as a result of which the existing economic system is overthrown through a revolution and a new system is set up; but that, in turn, leads to further class confrontation, and so the process continues. Marx looked towards the achievement of a classless society, where there would be no more confrontation, but where working people would own the means of production and distribution. This classless society would therefore be characterized by economic justice, in which each benefited from his or her own labour.

This was linked to his view of the fulfilment of the human individual. Marx argued that, in a capitalist system, an individual who works for a wage, producing something from which someone else is going to make a profit, becomes alienated from that working situation. He or she cannot exercise true creativity or humanity, but becomes an impersonal 'thing', a machine whose sole purpose in life is production, a means of making 'capital'. He saw this process leading to more and more wealth being concentrated in the hands of a small number of people, the 'bourgeoisie', with the working proletariat sinking into poverty. This, he believed, would eventually lead to the overthrow of the capitalist system by the workers acting together. He believed that, with the advent of the classless society, each individual would be able to develop to his or her full potential.

JUSTICE

The idea of justice is fundamental to political philosophy. If people are to band together for mutual protection, if they are to enter into social contracts, if they are to set their own interests aside, they need to be persuaded that the society within which they live is based on principles that are just. But what constitutes political justice?

We shall look at ideas of justice presented by three philosophers, one ancient and two modern.

PLATO

The question 'What is justice?' dominates one of the greatest works of philosophy, Plato's *Republic*. In this book (presented as a dialogue between Socrates and the representatives of contemporary schools of thought), various answers are proposed and rejected, as, for example, the popular but rather cynical view that justice is whatever is in the interest of the stronger! Plato recognizes that human nature can be deeply selfish, and that – given the opportunity to act with absolute impunity – people will generally seek their own benefit rather than that of others, or of society as a whole, and also explores the idea (later to be developed by the 'social contract' theory) that people need to be restrained for the good of all. But what is the value of justice in itself?

Socrates considers the various classes of people that make up the city, and argues that each class offers particular virtues, but that justice is found in the fact that each class performs its own task. In the same way, the individual soul is divided into three parts – mind, spirit and appetite – and that justice for the individual consists in the balance, with each part performing its own task for the benefit of that individual.

Justice is seen in the harmony and proper functioning of each part of society, and Plato wanted the rulers of his republic to be philosophers, seeking only the truth rather than their own self-interest. This, he argued, would be necessary if justice was to be established for all rather than in the interests of a particular section of the population.

Every philosophy needs to be seen against the background of its particular time and society, and Plato is no exception. His concept of a state ruled by philosophers, seeking a balance between elements in society and in the self, with priority given to the intellectual faculty, is not easily translatable into a modern political context. What is clear, however, is that justice (for Plato) is seen neither in equality (he never envisaged a society of equals) nor in sectional interest (he rejected the idea that it was the interest of the stronger), but in a balance in which different people and classes, each doing what is appropriate for them, work together for the common good.

RAWLS (JUSTICE AS FAIRNESS)

In *A Theory of Justice* (1972) John Rawls considers (as a thought experiment) a situation in which a group of people come together to decide the principles upon which their political association should operate. In other words, they set about forming a social contract. But he adds one further important criterion: that they should forget everything about themselves as individuals. They do not know if they are poor or wealthy, men or women. They do not know their race or their position within society. They come together simply as individuals, nothing more.

In other words, they are concerned to benefit themselves, but do not know who they are. By this means, Rawls hopes to achieve justice, for people will seek to legislate in a way that will benefit themselves, whoever they eventually turn out to be.

Rawls argues that such a group would require two principles:

1 **Liberty:** Each person should have equal rights to as extensive a set of basic liberties as possible, as long as that does not prevent others from having a similar set of fundamental liberties.

2 **Distribution of resources:** Given that there are social inequalities, Rawls argues that the distribution of resources should be such that the least advantaged in society receive the greatest benefit.

This is justice based on 'fairness'. Rawls argues that it is fair to grant everyone equal freedom and opportunity, and that, if there is to be inequality at all, it should only be allowed on the grounds that it benefits those who have the least advantages in life. The task of society (in addition to the basic protection of individuals who have come together to form it) is, according to Rawls, that it should organize the fair sharing out of both material and social benefits.

'I'm to give you a head start': the Rawlsian notion of justice

By making the people who come together to establish the principles of society forget who they are, they also relinquish all that they might naturally have gained and achieved. The successful person is made to forget all that he or she has gained by hard work, and to opt for an equal share of the pooled resources for fear of finding out that he or she was, in fact, the poorest.

In theory, this might establish a society where all are offered fair shares. But could it work like that in the real world? It could be argued that there never was, and never will be, an 'original position' from which to devise the rules of a society. All actual legal systems, and all ideas of justice, are framed within, and grow out of, an historical context.

NOZICK (JUSTICE AS ENTITLEMENT)

If the purpose of society is to protect the life, liberty and property of individuals, then each person should be enabled to retain those things which are rightly theirs. A society which, in the name of establishing equality, redistributes that wealth is in fact depriving an individual of the very protection which led to the formation of society in the first place.

This approach to the question of justice is taken by Robert Nozick. In *Anarchy, State and Utopia* (1974), he argued that it is wrong for the state to take taxes from individuals or force them to contribute to a health service that benefits others. It infringes their liberty to gain wealth and retain it. For Nozick, it is perfectly right to give what you have to another person if you so choose, but not to demand that another person give to you. On this social theory, voluntary contributions are welcomed, but enforced taxes are not. He argues that justice is a matter of the entitlement of individuals to retain their 'holdings' – wealth that they have gained legitimately.

FREEDOM AND LAW

Freedom in this context means something rather different from the 'freedom/determinism' debate outlined earlier. In that case, the determinist argument was that everything depends on prior causes and may (in theory) be predicted scientifically. Hence we are never free to choose what we do, even if our lack of understanding of the determining causes means that we retain the illusion of freedom.

Here, the debate is about the degree of freedom that the individual has a right to exercise within society, given the impact that such freedom may have upon the freedom of others: freedom to act within certain parameters set out by the law. Once a person acts outside those parameters, society, through the police and the courts, can step in and impose a penalty on the 'outlaw'.

Taking a utilitarian view of morality (see Friday), J.S. Mill argued that, in the case of some private matter, where an action and its consequences affect only the individual concerned, there should be absolute freedom. The law should step in to restrain that freedom only when the consequences of an action affects other people. This is the common-sense basis for much legislation.

HUMAN RIGHTS

In an ideal society, the law would always be framed on the basis of the agreement between free individuals, and every person would be equally free to enjoy basic human rights. There is, however, a difference between having a set of rights and being free to exercise those rights. In general, even though rights are given irrespective of age and capacities, it is sometimes necessary for the exercise of those rights to be curtailed:

- **On grounds of age.** Children have rights, and are protected by the law from exploitation by others, but cannot, for example, buy cigarettes or alcohol, drive a car or fly a plane. These limits are imposed because, below the relevant age, the child is considered unable to take a responsible decision and parents, or society, therefore impose a restriction on the child's freedom.
- **On grounds of insanity.** Those who are insane and are liable to be a danger to themselves or to others are also restrained.
- **On grounds of lack of skill.** Flying a plane or driving a car (other than on private property) without a licence is illegal. This can be justified on utilitarian grounds, since others in the air or on the roads could be in danger. Equally, to pose as a surgeon and perform operations without the appropriate qualification is illegal. Without the public acknowledgement that a person has the required skills, many such tasks would endanger the lives or wellbeing of others.

Rights are also taken from those who break the law, for example:

- through prison sentences
- through legal injunctions to stop actions being carried out or to prevent one person from approaching another or visiting a particular place. This may be taken retrospectively, if a person has already broken a law, or proactively, for example, to stop publication of a potentially damaging story in a newspaper.

In all these cases, a person retains his or her fundamental rights, but cannot exercise them, on the basis that to do so would be against the interests of society as a whole. This approach is based on the idea of a social contract, where the laws of society are made by mutual agreement, and the loss of certain freedoms are exchanged for the gain of a measure of social protection. It may also therefore be justified on utilitarian grounds.

FEMINISM

It may not have escaped the notice of many readers that almost all the philosophers mentioned so far in this book are male. The agenda, both philosophically and politically, appears to have been set by men, and the rational and legal approaches to many issues seem particularly appropriate to a male intellectual environment, but may be thought to ignore the distinctive contribution of women.

Feminism, therefore, introduces the issue of gender into the concepts of justice, fairness and rights, pointing out those areas where men have sought to exclude or marginalize women. A key work in the campaign on behalf of women was Mary Wollstonecraft's *A Vindication of the Rights of Women* (1792), where she argued for equality on the grounds of intellect. This did not imply that there should be no distinction between men and women, however, and she was quite happy to see women and men play very different roles within society. In fact, she saw women as primarily contributing from within the home.

In the nineteenth century, the key issue for the feminist perspective on British political life was the campaign for women to receive the vote. This was not an issue presented only by women, for it received the support of J.S. Mill, the utilitarian philosopher.

Feminism has generally sought to present an historical critique of the social injustices suffered by women, suggesting that gender bias is not simply a matter of individual prejudice, but is inherent in social and political institutions. On a broader front, it has also opened up discussion on the relationship between the sexes, the distinctive role of women, and the ethical implications of gender. Notable here is the contribution of Simone de Beauvoir (1908–86), the existentialist philosopher. Her book *The Second Sex* (1949) opened up a serious consideration of the myths and roles that women were expected to play within society, as mothers, wives, lovers and so on, and of their place in society. Perhaps her most famous quote 'One is not born, but rather becomes a woman' suggested that the roles of womanhood were imposed upon women (by a male-dominated society), rather than being essential to her nature.

SUMMARY

In today's chapter we have looked at another rich branch of philosophy, one with a tradition that dates back to Plato's *Republic* and Aristotle's *Politics*. Above all, we have focused on thinkers whose ideas have helped shape modern Western democracy. Thus, we have traced the development of the social contract, through thinkers such as Hobbes and Locke; the ideas of Karl Marx, notably dialectic materialism; and finally the competing notions of justice as presented by Rawls and Nozick. All of these thinkers have had a profound impact on actual political practice – for instance Locke on the development of representative democracy, Rawls on the liberal Left, and Nozick on the libertarian Right.

This has been a busy, crowded week and we have been able to gain only glimpses into what is an enormous and diverse subject. While ethics and political philosophy – the most obviously 'practical' branches of the discipline – occupy the foreground in much contemporary philosophical discourse, I hope that I have shown that other areas of

SUNDAY

MONDAY

TUESDAY

WEDNESDAY

THURSDAY

FRIDAY

SATURDAY

philosophy – from the philosophy of mind to the philosophy of language – are similarly rich in challenging and thought-provoking ideas and have an impact that reverberates across the whole spectrum of human endeavour.

FACT-CHECK (ANSWERS AT THE BACK)

1. What did Thomas Hobbes see as a fundamental human need?
   a) Self-interest ☐
   b) Self-preservation ☐
   c) Self-improvement ☐
   d) Self-esteem ☐

2. In what major work did Hobbes lay out his ideas?
   a) *Leviticus* ☐
   b) *Leviathan* ☐
   c) *Levity and Law* ☐
   d) None of the above ☐

3. In what major respect did Locke differ from Hobbes?
   a) The right to liberty ☐
   b) The right to private property ☐
   c) The right of the ruled to replace their ruler ☐
   d) The right to equality ☐

4. Marx was influenced above all by which philosopher?
   a) Kant ☐
   b) Feuerbach ☐
   c) Herder ☐
   d) Hegel ☐

5. In what major way did Marx interpret the dialectical progress of history? For him, it was primarily about...
   a) Spiritual advancement ☐
   b) Class war ☐
   c) Material change ☐
   d) The extension of human rights ☐

6. In Plato's ideal republic, which group of people would rule?
   a) Artists ☐
   b) Philosophers ☐
   c) Aristocrats ☐
   d) Everyone ☐

7. Which two principles lie at the heart of Rawls's theory of justice?
   a) Liberty ☐
   b) Legality ☐
   c) Equality ☐
   d) Distribution of resources ☐

8. What is at the heart of Nozick's idea about justice?
   a) The right to make money ☐
   b) The right to have property ☐
   c) The right to keep what is lawfully gained ☐
   d) The right to equality ☐

9. On what grounds is it usually considered acceptable to curtail the exercise of human rights?
   a) Age ☐
   b) Gender ☐
   c) Skill ☐
   d) Insanity ☐

10. Historically, philosophy has...
    a) Been gender neutral ☐
    b) Marginalized women ☐
    c) Been dominated by male thinkers ☐
    d) All of the above ☐

AFTERWORD

THE SCOPE OF PHILOSOPHY TODAY

During the twentieth century there were a number of movements that attempted to reduce philosophy to some other discipline. The positivists wanted philosophy to follow science, throwing out all that did not conform to empirical criteria of meaning. Then the linguistic analysts insisted that the whole task of philosophy was the unpacking of statements to clarify their meaning. Marxists wanted everything reduced to its social and political matrix, and postmodernists saw everything in terms of cultural and literary metaphors or signs, strung together. One might imagine that philosophy would be shaken radically by such drastic criticisms and reinterpretations of its task, but this has not been the case.

For anyone coming to philosophy at the end of the 1950s, however, at least in university departments concentrating on the Anglo-American analytic tradition, the task and scope of philosophy was precise but narrow. Still dominated by linguistic analysis, it aimed to examine problematic sentences and, through their elucidation, clarify meaning. It did not aspire to offer any new information on any subject. It saw itself as a necessary aid to all other subjects, rather than having a subject content of its own.

Over the last 50 years, however, philosophy has seen remarkable growth, both in its popularity as a subject and in the range and relevance of the topics it covers. One impetus for change came initially within the area of applied ethics. In the days of linguistic analysis, everything was focused on the meaning or otherwise of ethical propositions, and it was quite reasonable for a philosopher to claim to have nothing to say about moral issues themselves. But it was increasingly recognized that ethical guidance was needed by professionals, particularly in medicine and nursing, in order to develop and implement standards for dealing with the many difficult moral questions raised in their everyday work. Questions about abortion and euthanasia, the use of drugs and the conduct of medical research, all needed to be answered by sound moral arguments based on accepted professional standards.

Philosophy in the boardroom

At the same time, the rise of the cognitive sciences, information technology and artificial intelligence has raised questions about the nature of mind. International politics grapples with concepts – democracy, human rights, self-determination, national sovereignty – to direct and justify its action or inaction in various crises. Political philosophy is therefore utterly relevant to the human agenda. Issues concerning the philosophy of art – censorship, copyright, what distinguishes valid erotic art from pornography, what constitutes 'taste' or blasphemy, the nature of artistic expression – may be relevant when an art prize is judged, or when artists produce images that some find inspiring and others want banned. Relevant here also are legal debates about the ownership of intellectual property, about who should be paid royalties or claim copyright on ideas and words. Social awareness brings with it issues of feminism and of race, of inequality and the dynamics of free markets.

With the Internet comes a whole raft of issues about self-expression, privacy, international controls, exploitation and the nature of communication. In a complex world, something more is needed of philosophy than the mere clarification of meaning. *Even beyond the obvious area of ethics, philosophy is increasingly becoming 'applied'.* And it is therefore also becoming more obviously relevant to everyday life – it is the subject for dealing with big questions.

Without doubt, philosophy as an academic discipline is alive and well, but the first decade of the twenty-first century has seen another phenomenon – the explosion of interest in 'popular' philosophy. Books by philosophers on a whole range of subjects, but particularly those related to human self-understanding and self-development, are increasingly produced for the general reader, rather than for the academic specialist. The nature of status, or of love, of justice or of commitment, of work, or of all the elements that go to make up the art of living, all require thoughtful reflection, and philosophy provides the discipline for doing just that.

Perhaps the last word should come from a traditional metaphysical philosopher, writing early in the twentieth century. In *Modes of Thought* (1938), A.N. Whitehead set down very clearly the value of the whole philosophical enterprise:

> *The sort of ideas we attend to, and the sort of ideas we push into the negligible background, govern our hopes, our fears, our control of behaviour. As we think, we live. This is why the assemblage of philosophical ideas is more than a specialist study. It moulds our type of civilization.*

If that is so, there is nothing more important than developing and maintaining an interest in philosophy.

GLOSSARY

analytic Used to describe a statement that is true by definition (and thus in a sense tautological); *compare* **synthetic**

a posteriori Known to be true by virtue of experience; *compare* **a priori**

a priori Known to be true prior to and independent of experience; *compare* **a posteriori**

categorical imperative In Kantian ethics, the absolute moral principle that one's behaviour should accord with universally valid maxims

cognition The metal process by which knowledge is acquired

dialectic materialism The political and economic philosophy of Karl Marx by which society progresses by resolving opposite economic forces

dualism In the philosophy of mind, where body and mind are believed to be separate but causally linked

empiricism The belief that all knowledge derives from the senses

epistemology The theory or philosophy of knowledge and how it is acquired

ethics The branch of philosophy concerned with describing and deciding the values and moral principles that should govern human conduct

idealism The notion that everything that exists is mental

logic Branch of philosophy concerned with using systematic patterns of reasoning to draw conclusions

logical positivism Twentieth-century school of philosophy that held that factual statements could be known to be true only if backed by actual or possible evidence

materialism The notion that everything is explicable in terms of physical phenomena

metaphysics Branch of philosophy concerned with the ultimate nature of reality

noumenon (pl.: -mena) In Kantian thought, a thing as it exists in itself independent of our experience of it; *compare* **phenomenon**

phenomenon (pl.: -mena) In Kantian thought, a thing as perceived; *compare* **noumenon**

pragmatism Philosophical stance that holds that we should (provisionally) accept those theories that have the greater practical use

rationalism The belief that all knowledge derives from human reason; *compare* **empiricism**

scepticism In philosophy, the belief that absolute knowledge of reality is impossible, and that every statement may therefore be challenged

syllogism Process of logical thought in which two premises lead to a conclusion

synthetic Used to describe a statement that is true only if proved to be so by external evidence; *compare* **analytic**

utilitarianism Approach to ethics by which the rightness of an action is decided by the fruitfulness (or 'utility') of its consequences

ANSWERS

Sunday: 1a; 2d; 3d; 4b; 5d; 6c; 7b; 8d; 9c; 10d

Monday: 1d; 2c; 3a; 4d; 5c; 6b & d; 7a; 8c, d, b, a; 9b; 10b & d

Tuesday: 1b; 2d; 3b & c; 4b, c & d; 5c; 6c; 7b & c; 8a & b; 9b; 10c

Wednesday: 1c; 2b (and possibly c also); 3d; 4b & d (but arguably all four!); 5c & d; 6c; 7c & a; 8c; 9a, b, c & d; 10b

Thursday: 1b & c; 2b & c; 3d; 4b; 5d; 6b; 7c; 8a & c; 9b; 10b

Friday: 1a, b, c & d; 2c & d; 3a; 4a & c; 5d; 6d; 7d; 8d; 9a, b & d; 10b

Saturday: 1b; 2b; 3c; 4d; 5c; 6b; 7a & d; 8c; 9a, c & d; 10b & c